The
New Science
and Spirituality
Reader

The New Science and Spirituality Reader

EDITED BY ERVIN LASZLO

AND

KINGSLEY L. DENNIS

Inner Traditions

Rochester, Vermont • Toronto, Canada

Inner Traditions
One Park Street
Rochester, Vermont 05767
www.InnerTraditions.com

Text stock is SFI certified

Library of Congress Cataloging-in-Publication Data is available
The new science and spirituality reader / edited by Ervin Laszlo and Kingsley L.
Dennis.
    p. cm.
  Includes index.
  Summary: "Bridging the gap between science and the world's great spiritual
traditions to move our worldview forward"—Provided by publisher.
   ISBN 978-1-59477-476-8 (pbk.) — ISBN 978-1-59477-687-8 (e-book)

Printed and bound in the United States by Lake Book Manufacturing, Inc.
The text stock is SFI certified. The Sustainable Forestry Initiative® program
promotes sustainable forest management.

10 9 8 7 6 5 4 3 2 1

Text design by Jon Desautels
Text layout by Virginia Scott Bowman
This book was typeset in Garamond Premier Pro with Agenda and Copperplate
used as display typefaces

To send correspondence to the author of this book, mail a first-class letter to the
author c/o Inner Traditions • Bear & Company, One Park Street, Rochester, VT
05767, and we will forward the communication, or visit the author's website at
www.worldshiftinternational.org or **www.kingsleydennis.com**.

Contents

ROUND THREE

Searching for the Meeting Ground

ROUND FOUR

Stepping-Stones toward Unification

Foreword

DEEPAK CHOPRA

This groundbreaking collection of essays is not what it appears. Fortunately, it is much more. On the surface, the hot button topic of science versus religion has grown cooler recently, once a small band of vociferous atheists had their moment in the spotlight. Another book arguing that science and religion should be allies instead of foes would help to heal a public rift. Yet what rift really exists, and how much does it matter? In their private lives, scientists attend church more often than the average responder to polls. Five hundred years after the rise of science and the gradual waning of religion, there's not much spice left in the debate.

What remains is far more fascinating. In a way that few people realize, science has reached a wall that it cannot break through. After rationality seemed to render religion more or less useless as a way to explain how nature works, scientists wound up with nothing less than a mystic's universe. In this universe, the entire cosmos emerged from a complete void. *Something* gave rise to time and space, yet it exists beyond time and space. *Something* has organized creation with such precision that the slightest tremor in the governing laws of nature would mean that the Big Bang was a Big Flop. As little as one part in a billion of mass-energy in the first instant of the cosmos (by instant I mean a tenth of a second followed by forty-three zeroes) would have caused an implosion back into the realm of "dark" matter and energy. As it is, 95 percent of the infant universe did collapse back into that unknown realm.

Something is doing far more even than this. It allowed the conditions for consciousness to arise. It set in motion an evolutionary unfolding that began with hydrogen atoms 13.7 billion years ago and arrived at the human brain, the most complex structure in the known universe. *Something* balanced the forces of creation and destruction in so delicate a fashion that a hyper-intricate molecule like DNA, which would dry up and blow away if exposed to sunlight on a hot summer day, has remained intact for more than two billion years.

In the face of these facts, science has come to a crossroads—and not just science. Each of us must consider what it means to live inside an illusion, because that is what the physical universe is. The atom, which serves as the basis for all matter, has no physical properties. It is composed of energy patterns emerging from invisible fields, and those fields exist primarily in a virtual state—meaning that they aren't even present in the physical universe.

Or to encapsulate the present state of our knowledge: *What's the matter? Nothing. Literally nothing.*

Living in an illusion poses only two choices: either you face the fact that reality must be redefined or you turn away and try to forget that ordinary existence is based on nothingness. That's a strong choice, and workaday science can be forgiven for ignoring the illusion. After all, thousands of researchers and technicians go to their laboratories like anyone else going to work. They run experiments without regard for the illusory nature of life, which can be set aside as metaphysics. Such an attitude has reached the end of its viability, however.

The wall that science now faces cannot be ignored, because on the other side lies the ultimate prize, the Theory of Everything that has long been the fabled unicorn of physics. Mainstream physicists have ironically called one of the elusive building blocks of nature "the God particle" (as the Higgs boson* was nicknamed). One camp of cosmologists—by far the largest—hopes to penetrate the deepest recesses of nature through the same old means, ratcheting up super colliders and billion-dollar space telescopes to extend the five senses farther than ever before.

A smaller camp takes a different view, pointing out that if the universe emerged from a void, if nothing is the basis of everything, and if dark matter and energy turn out to be the controlling forces of the cosmos, maybe we are in mystical territory already. Instead of struggling against the principles that bind together the world's wisdom traditions, an expanded science needs to see if they are valid. In particular, there is every reason to accept that the universe is a conscious, living, evolving, and creative being. Or, if "being" is too strange a word, we can substitute "process." The process that gave rise to human life appears to be non-random; it is self-organizing and self-regulating. Once this notion is accepted, many huge difficulties suddenly disappear.

I won't give away what those difficulties are: let the far-seeing contributors to this collection unfold them. Instead I'd like to clarify three terms that appear on every page of this book. The first is *religion*. Every writer here, whether aligned with science or spirituality, is not arguing for traditional religious teachings. None is boosting God or tearing him down. In a broader sense, the subject has moved beyond religion to spirituality, which is the second term we need to clarify. *Spirituality* is the essence of every faith, yet it is contained by no single faith. It has to do with invisible things like the soul, numen ("an influence perceptible by mind but not by senses"), atman, pleroma, and Shekinah.

But thumbing through a Rolodex of traditional terms doesn't bring us closer to what science needs right now. Spirituality, if it is going to bridge two worldviews, must focus on something that everyone can accept as real, if only provisionally. My favored candidate is consciousness.

---

*The Higgs boson is a hypothetical elementary particle that has zero spin and large mass and that is required by some gauge theories to account for the masses of other elementary particles.

Spirituality is the domain of consciousness, embracing the observer, the observed, and the process of observation. In updated language, that's how Vedanta, the deepest branch of Indian spirituality, defines itself. But no one is being urged to accept a single definition. Spirituality is flexible, lenient, and expandable. The reader will be able to pick up any essay in this book and apply his own definition—no harm done.

The third term to clarify is *mysticism*. I'm guilty of using it here without a definition, and there's a danger that two different people will see mysticism as either highest truth or utter nonsense. The only value in using the word at all is that it gathers into one corral a host of inspired guides, teachers, and writers such as Plato, Rumi, St. John of the Cross, Lao-tzu, and Rabindranath Tagore. To be mystical is to experience the soul, or by any other name the source, the essence, and the presence of transcendent reality. To be mystical is to go beyond the world of appearance. That is the common task of science and spirituality today. If they are successful in going beyond, we will enter a phase where separate realities will fuse into a single reality. One camp may call it the Theory of Everything while the other calls it the experience of everything. Reality won't mind.

Every writer in this book aims to bring such a day closer, and it's heartening that so many diverse minds have caught glimpses of one reality. I doubt that there will be a banner day in the future when the ultimate breakthrough is announced and all parties are reconciled. But it would be even better if one day a scientist could read the following lines from Tagore and nod in silent agreement:

> *I grew tired of the road*
> *when it took me here and there.*
> *I married it in love*
> *when it took me everywhere.*

Introduction

The Alliance of Science and Spirituality at a Time of Crisis and Transformation

A deep gulf separates science and spirituality today. This is an unfortunate development: in classical times the dominant culture encompassed both rational and spiritual elements, as it still does in some Eastern and traditional societies to this day. The mechanistic, materialistic, and rational view of a nonliving, clockwork universe that was born out of the Enlightenment helped humanity to free itself from superstition and to achieve incredible scientific breakthroughs. While we do acknowledge this, we must also recognize, and accept, that this paradigm no longer serves human evolution. In modern society, in fact, the gulf between science and spirituality has given rise to what is akin to a "dialogue of the deaf," or perhaps rather what English physicist and novelist C. P. Snow called "the two cultures": the culture of the scientists and the culture of the humanists. The scientists often consider the ideas and worldviews of the humanists' armchair philosophy and mere wishful thinking, while the humanists are prone to believing that they have access to a dimension of reality about which scientists have nothing to say. These dialectical positions have hardened into a veritable tug-of-war

1

where neither side is willing to cede an inch or even listen to the other.

This situation fragments the contemporary world and produces animosity and tension, culminating at its worst in fundamentalism and violence. And it gives us blindfolds that prevent us from seeing a wider, fuller picture, a reality sourced in the best insights of science as well as spirituality.

What we need to consider is that there is no evolution, no shift, without an element of spirituality. We cannot have a shift that is purely rational, nor can we do it also purely by intuition and spirituality. It is necessary to foster an alliance between science and the great traditions of spiritual wisdom. Humanity is not only a collective of rational beings; inherent to us also is the element of gnosis, of the inner connection to a deep source of nourishment and, for many, guidance. If we can bring these two aspects together we can form a broader, more integral understanding of the world around us. With a combination of science and spirituality we can move beyond a purely sense-driven perception of our environment into a more expansive perception of how we are connected to a world, a universe, at a deeper, more fundamental level.

Through spirituality we are able to perceive connections that are otherwise unavailable through solely rational, scientific means. Similarly, through science we are able to learn how physical and energetic connections arise and are maintained. Also, with the very latest findings in quantum physics we are seeing a closer convergence between what has been taught for generations in the wisdom traditions and what is arising under the most advanced scientific observations. What we are discovering is that every part of what is in existence is intrinsically connected within the fabric of the whole. If we can bring this knowledge together and realize that science can verify this, we can begin to close the artificial gap that has existed for too long—the gap that categorizes a person as either a follower of science or as a "spiritual dreamer." This dangerous gap is indeed being dissolved as we move into the twenty-first century by the new sciences that are recognizing that the insights of spirituality have a real basis within the physical universe. Likewise, our modern understanding of spirituality is mature enough to recognize that we have tremendous faculties of reason and rational inquiry and that together both these aspects of human nature are able to form a more completed human being, more capable of taking charge of the responsibilities required to participate in our inner and outer evolution.

Humanity is involved in a collective journey that is unfolding around us at an accelerating pace. Much will be asked of us, and much will be expected. It does not matter what our individual and varied religious, spiritual, philosophical, social, or any other beliefs are. We are being called on to embrace our unity rather than our differences, to practice our sense of integrity and decency, and to develop trust in a new type of vision for the way forward. This clearly involves too a unity in our areas of understanding and perception, as the dualistic mode of thinking that has brought us to our current impasse is now fostering our crises.

Through reevaluating our knowledge base in line with what the new sciences reveal to us about the nature of reality, we may be better equipped with the right tools to make sense of a more expansive, creative reality, and to reconnect once again to a living universe. Yet if we wish to stimulate this reconnecting process then we need to reevaluate our current ideas and beliefs. Our fragmented world picture of duality, conflict, strife, and discord no longer supports the place where we need to be. At the same time we also need to have the courage to face what is manifesting in our lives in order to transform those moments within our very selves. Through bridging the gap between scientific thought and spiritual gnosis we have a more profound platform in which to address our most pressing concerns: a conscious evolutionary worldshift. The impulse for such a worldshift is not only imperative, it is also an evolutionary necessity.

Let us be clear about our current situation: our planet is experiencing a converging set of crises that together may very likely catalyze drastic and radical change within our social, political, geological, and religious systems. Within such critical moments there are potential trigger points of social unrest and uncertainty that can either sway in the favor of a breakthrough or breakdown. However, whether this will be a smooth ride or not will depend largely on our individual and collective mind-sets and actions.

Within us we have the capacity to facilitate a perceptual shift within our various social realities; we can, literally, "change our minds." To encourage this we may wish to consider the latest information being revealed by the new sciences: the fields of quantum physics, quantum biology, and biophysics. These scientific investigations are now revealing to us the underlying realities enforcing our sense of reality. They tell us how we are connected energetically and consciously and how we possess the capacity for activating vital energies of development. In this sense we are not a completed species: we are still evolving and developing, and there exists the possibility that we can influence this process so that change can occur within an individual lifetime rather than between generations.

Part of this change—this *worldshift*—may come through a new form of sociospiritual renaissance that has been slowing gestating within our cultures and societies for generations and that is now emerging. This renewal may be experienced through reevaluating our social networks, relationships, lifestyles, and communities as well as securing a more harmonious connection with our environment and resources.

We are not lacking in the creative vision and energies needed to shift into a more harmonious and sustainable global future for the planet and ourselves. There is enough available creative energy to support the human venture, especially when it is expressed through positive collaborative sharing and a more integral worldview. Our sacred story is now one of integration and collaboration, not one of fragmentation and competition.

Our new narrative is now one of an evolving species within an evolving universe, which can be a great adventure that is both irreversible and creatively new. As intermediaries we can integrate scientific knowledge with spiritual insight so that real work can be done that benefits all of humanity and all of Earth's living creatures and living systems. Modern science has confirmed the unity of humans within a living and energetic environment. It is important that we allow this to form a new integral way of thinking that seeks to converge rather than fragment.

With this book that you now hold in your hands—*The New Science and Spirituality Reader*—we hope to assist this very necessary "two cultures" dialogue through promoting new-paradigm thinking and acting. The schism between science and spirituality is not only an historical and sociopolitical division, it is also a perceptual one. Our perceptual frameworks, and hence our cultural realities, are structured through the limitations as well as the vision of our human thinking. Our perception of reality depends on our "habits of perception," which we develop throughout our lives. These perceptual habits—or *markers*—are often constructed and/or validated through the sociocultural institutions of a given era. To move on, to break with these perceptual habits and push for an emerging new paradigm of thought, requires from us that we are open to questioning our frameworks of belief and knowledge. By not questioning the existing structures of belief and knowledge—in this case, science and spirituality—we are forfeiting our right to consciously evolve our patterns of understanding.

This book (which first began life as the Ervin Laszlo Forum on Science & Spirituality—www.ervinlaszlo.com/forum), is based on an invitation for leading exponents of the scientific and the humanistic cultures to engage in insightful and inspiring conversation. It does not intend to convince one culture of the truth of the other. It grants to the humanists that scientists cannot explain the full dimensions of genuine spirituality and may never do so. But it grants to the scientists that their theories are not as irrelevant to the spiritual experience as humanists tend to claim. All we know of the world comes to us through experience, and human experience has more facets than either side is willing to grant to the other. To grasp a few more of these facets would go a long way toward a meeting of the minds—a meeting that is not the victory of one side over the other, but the victory of insight and understanding over dogma and prejudice.

The gulf between science and spirituality need not prove unbridgeable. But like bridge building in the real world, construction has to start on solid ground on both sides of the divide. For this reason the editors of this book have invited open-minded and credible scientists and humanists to describe their own views of the world and the experiences on which they are based. These conversations, followed up through seminars and symposia, are to lead in time to a broader dialogue that substitutes understanding for prejudice and makes a meaningful contribution to healing the rift that fragments the modern world.

This book is especially timely because humanity is now experiencing a period of crisis and transformation. It is a time in our history when we are forced into reflecting on our value systems and modes of thought. In other words, we are in the throes of a profound and potentially promising *worldshift*. Yet in order for a worldshift to come about we need to catalyze rapid change in how we act in the world. For this to occur, we need first to create a shift in our perceptual paradigms. Every one of us lives as part of an interconnected, whole-system world, yet many of us continue to act as if we were separate entities, out to please only ourselves and ready to subordinate everything and everybody in the material quest for an instant accumulation of wealth and power. As a species, this means a loss of coherence, which translates as a loss of viability. For humanity to shift its present direction, we need to engage in a dialogue on some of our most fundamental issues of our life and existence.

The twenty-first century is the meeting point where the wisdom of ancient traditions can find a synthesis with modern science. Our knowledge systems are converging to help us synthesize and make use of our resources, to help us advance and continue forward. This book is a small contribution to this developing—and profoundly important—debate.

The Shared Essence of Science and Spirituality

Introduction to Round One

Two famous scientists and two renowned spiritual leaders are the protagonists of our opening round. Medical doctor and eminent wellness advisor Deepak Chopra speaks of a war between religion and science and wisely seeks to steer clear of its worst expressions: the claims of those who try to defend religion and spirituality by attacking science and the claims of those who try to defend science by attacking spirituality. Chopra notes that the war must, and ultimately will, find resolution in the recognition that at the base of both science and spirituality there is consciousness and that a true understanding of consciousness will show that there is no conflict between them. Consciousness is primary; it's the ground of all we experience. Following this discussion the distinguished physical scientist Rustum Roy points an accusing finger at those misguided and critical scientific voices that, he claims, do not come from real scientists and do not represent the bulk of the working science community. Such grossly imprecise, sloppy statements amount to no less than a crime in Roy's thinking.

Next, we have two eminent spiritual thinkers who approach this issue from the other side by testifying that the religious and spiritual experience is real and credible. World-renowned spiritual guide Jean Houston outlines how anyone who is ready and willing can enter into these deeper domains of the psyche that, at their deepest level, make up the mystical experience. Her affirmation is echoed and illuminated by charismatic spiritual leader Michael Beckwith. Just as Houston speaks of the "mystical experience," so Beckwith speaks of the experience of "extended awareness." He affirms that the spiritual realms of human experience are woven into the very fabric of our physical and biological existence.

Ultimately, spirituality and science come together in the realization that, at its deepest and most genuine expressions, our experience is an experience of the oneness that characterizes all of reality. Beckwith calls this the One Mind, and for scientists it's at the root of the coherence underlying all observed phenomena, a coherence that physicists searching for a "theory of everything" seek to express in a master formula similar to, yet still more embracing than, Einstein's famous $E = mc^2$.

So, we start by acknowledging the war between spirituality and science and demonstrate how confusion and discord reign supreme, but we end by focusing squarely on the legitimacy of spiritual experience and the desperate need for a science based on its exploration.

1

Consciousness and the End of the War between Science and Religion

DEEPAK CHOPRA

Nothing gets as vicious as fighting for a lost cause. If the proverbial Martian landed in a flying saucer today and saw how religionists war against scientists, he would be surprised at the vehemence on both sides. What is the war about? Fact beat out faith long ago. When Darwin's theory of evolution replaced Genesis to explain the appearance of human beings, which was in the middle of the nineteenth century, the trend away from faith was already old. The world had been remade as material, governed by natural laws, random in its effects, and immune to divine intervention. Not just science but also thousands of unanswered prayers did their part to dethrone God.

I am not drawn to lost causes, and therefore I'd like to guide the debate away from religion. And since religion is the primary form of spirituality in most people's lives, we'll have to step away from spirituality, too, at least at first. There should be renewed admiration for science's attempts to answer the fundamental mysteries. These are well known by now:

How did the universe come about?

What caused life to emerge from a soup of inorganic chemicals?

Can evolution explain all of human development?

What are the basic forces in nature?

How does the brain produce intelligence?

What place do human beings occupy in the cosmos?

Many observers have linked these questions to spirituality, too. Facts tell us how life came about, but faith still wants to know why. But what strikes me is how useless these big questions easily become. You and I live our lives without asking them. We may be philosophically curious; we may even have enough leisure time to reflect on the big picture. For all that, the big questions are posed, by and large, by professors who are paid to pose them. Religion and science occupy different kinds of ivory towers, but until they come down to earth, neither one meets the practical needs of life.

Science comes down to earth as technology; religion comes down to earth as comfort. But viewed together, they fall short of a common factor that guides every moment of daily life: consciousness. The future of spirituality will converge with the future of science when we actually know how and why we think, what makes us alive to the outer and inner worlds, and how we came to be so rich in creativity. Being alive is inconceivable without being conscious. "I think, therefore I am" is fundamentally true, but Descartes' maxim should be expanded to include feeling, intuition, a sense of self, and our drive to understand who we are.

The practical application of consciousness seems remote compared with technology. Would you rather be enlightened or own an iPad? In modern society, the choice is all too obvious. But it's a false choice because people don't realize that the things they most cherish and desire are born in consciousness: love, happiness, freedom from fear, the absence of depression, and a vision of the future. We achieve all these things when consciousness is healthy, open, alert, and expansive. We lose them when consciousness is cramped, constricted, confused, and detached from its source.

I receive Google alerts every day telling me that one skeptic or another calls these considerations "woo." It's not my role to defeat skepticism, which amounts in practice to a conspiracy for the suppression of curiosity. Science advances through data and experiments, but those in turn depend on theory. Theory is the flashlight that tells an experimenter where to look, and without it, he wanders at random. His data don't fit into a worldview. I consider myself scientific at heart, and so I depend on a theory as well. Its basic premises are as follows:

We live in a universe that exhibits intelligence, self-regulation, and creativity.
Consciousness preceded the brain. It created life and went on to create the brain itself.
Consciousness is primary in the world; matter is secondary.
Evolution is conscious and therefore creative. It isn't random.
At the source of creation one finds a field of pure awareness.
Pure awareness is the source of every manifest quality in the universe.

Scientists don't use most of the terms that are central to my theory, which isn't mine, actually, but was born and sustained through the world's wisdom traditions. In the name of objectivity, science leaves consciousness out of its equations and is fiercely proud for doing so. In doing that, a scientist is pretending not to be part of life, as if thinking, feeling, creating, loving, and enmeshing oneself in the complexities of the inner world were all irrelevant.

In fact, nothing could be more relevant. While the general public sees atheists mounting windy charges against superstitious believers, neither side is moving forward. The future lies with anyone who seriously delves into consciousness. Why? Because with physics arriving at the quantum world, neuroscience at the most minuscule operations of brain cells, and biology at the finest fabrics of DNA, all three have hit a wall. At the finest level, nature is too complex to unravel through such weak ideas as randomness, materialism, and unconscious mechanics. Nature behaves, and as we know from ourselves, behavior is tricky. Science has tons of data about phenomena that don't fit any explanation. For example:

How does an observer cause light to change from acting like a wave to acting like a particle?

How can a group of ordinary people cause a random number generator to turn out more ones than zeros simply by wanting it to?

How do millions of monarch butterflies migrate to the same mountainous regions of Mexico when they've never been there before and were not born there?

How do twins connect at a distance, so that one knows immediately when the other has been hurt or dies?

Where in the brain does the self live? Why do I feel like myself and no one else?

These are alluring mysteries, like trailing bits of yarn that lead back to a big tangled ball. This book, with its open-minded questioning, can help in the untangling. Yet it spells doom if anyone, either believer or skeptic, falls back on the tired and dishonest ploys that fill the debate today, such as:

I already know the answer in advance, which makes you automatically wrong.

I disdain your beliefs.

You're a fraud with dishonest motives.

I only want to make you look bad.

You don't know as much science as I do, or perhaps none at all.

Speculative thinking is foolish, superstitious, or both.

I'm here to win, not to find out the truth.

2

J'Accuse

Fuzzy Science and Sloppy Journalists

RUSTUM ROY

J'accuse! I accuse! The sloppy media reporters have written on "science and religion" topics for generations with grossly imprecise and inaccurate statements amounting to crimes. As a practicing scientist for sixty years and someone who is known worldwide for my science, I produce data, hard facts (*not* my opinions) to make my contributions to science, industry, and posterity. In the mass-press treatment of science and religion topics, I am insulted by the absurd confrontations engineered by the black-and-white print and video media and the ridiculous self-anointed representations of the position of science we are exposed to from representatives of the most esoteric brands of science.

Who can be said to speak for science? First emblazon on your mind that science must have *experimentally verifiable* facts as its data.

Surely not the likes of Richard Dawkins, Daniel Dennett, Christopher Hitchens, and Sam Harris? Not one of them qualifies as any kind of (hard) scientist. Stephen Weinberg or Stephen Hawking, whom I respect enormously as brilliant experts in their fields, are distinguished enough in science. But astronomy and cosmology are not classical science.*

A worthy media person should surely demand some standards of achievements, some surveys, statistics, polls, and details of in how many and in what kinds of sciences a quoted expert has credentials. Never, never, never have I seen such in science and religion articles. J'accuse the media reporters of hiding their personal beliefs under such sloppy work, of selecting scientists in esoteric fields with a known bias and with zero knowledge of contemporary religion for a straw-man debate on science and religion.

I propose an "NCIS-type" approach, instead, as better science. *Get the facts first.* Who represents science? There are over 5.5 million engineers and scientists in the United States. Who does the real science, those whom the world recognizes as scientists? For example, I believe most citizens would accept designers and engineers from Intel, Kodak, or Caterpillar as scientists. There are approximately twenty thousand physicists and one hundred thousand chemists in the United States who qualify by title, largely in universities and sound research labs. Among these there are probably three thousand to five thousand theoretical physicists, astronomers, particle physicists, and such in the country. However good their science, can it fix a lightbulb?

Ben Stein, in his detailed, scientific critique of the current biased debate, unearthed amazing facts about some scientists' fanatic commitments. Although the movie was poorly named *Expelled,* it includes essential information to highlight facts on science and scientists. The Darwinists, largely funded in the United States approximately twenty years before the Nazis' rise in Germany, used gas chambers and furnaces to kill off handicapped citizens. It's true! All of this is documented in living color!

In Stein's movie, the tour guide explains that those who were so

---

*See Dr. James Gunn, *Science* 317 (September 20, 2007); for similar sentiments, see Nobel Laureate in Physics Philip W. Anderson, in *Superconductivity,* vol. 2, ed. R. D. Parks, 1347–48 (New York: Marcel Dekker, 1969).

dispatched were referred to as "useless eaters," not carrying their weight in the world. Is there a parallel here among "nonperforming" scientists who do not produce anything of *value to society*? "Useless scientists?"

To represent science, let's use the real, useful hard science from the last two hundred years that the public at large accepts as good and valuable: experiments on stuff you can touch and feel, results you can measure and repeat a dozen times in which friends' and competitors' experiments confirm or deny your work, and mainly—yes, mainly—something of value to society. That's what I have been trying to do for sixty years (visit Google for the records.) American citizens think the media are referring to *such* scientists and their fields when they see absurd headlines about scientists denying (yes, "deniers") the possibility of spiritual healing, previous lives, or eternal life. *Which* scientists? Who is checking the facts? What percentages of them are useless eaters compared with real hard scientists?

How come the deniers are never confronted and investigated by a reporter who has carefully gathered facts from senior scientific authorities. For example, what about Professor Larry Dossey's data on the huge percentage of doctors who pray with or for patients and about their belief in miracles? Why is the hard data for pure scientific and spiritual healing by the shamans of Hawaii compiled by Jeanne Achterberg, which are all recorded on MRI scans, never mentioned? Or the three decades of research and data collected by Professors Ian Stephenson and Jim Turner at the University of Virginia on reincarnation here and now, worldwide. Remember, in science one white crow destroys your theory that "all crows are black."

Real science and real religion (not theology) have done well together in describing overlapping views of reality. That is the biggest opportunity for twenty-first-century science.

Verbum sapientiae satis.

Therefore, j'accuse the U.S. media of irresponsible, unbelievably biased reporting.

3

Spirituality and the Meaning of Mysticism for Our Time

JEAN HOUSTON

What is real spirituality but the art of union with reality? Mysticism is a particularly focused part of spirituality; the mystic is a person who aims at and believes in the attainment of such a union. In its classical spiritual form it is a heroic journey, and valiant efforts are required to follow the path.

Many of the spiritual teachers of the world have likened our lives to "a sleep and a forgetting." The mystical path is predicated on awakening, on going off robot and abandoning lackluster passivity to engage in cocreation with vigor, attention, focus, and radiance, characteristics we might note we often find in our animal friends.

Thus the mystical variant of the spiritual experience is perhaps the greatest accelerator of evolutionary enhancement. Through this experience, as Ervin Laszlo has noted in his own writings on quantum consciousness, we tap into wider physical, mental, and emotional systems, thereby gaining entrance into the next stage of our unfolding, both individually and collectively. Once the province of the few, the spiritual experience, and within it the mystical path, may now be the requirement of the many—a unique developmental path for self and world.

In a lifetime of studying the art and science of human development, I have found no more powerful, practical, and evolutionary practice than the mystical path. When I have studied or talked with seekers who have had this variety of the spiritual experience, they have told me of a joy that passes understanding, an immense surge of creativity, an instant up-rush of kindness and tolerance that makes them impassioned champions for the betterment of all, bridge builders, magnets for solutions, peacemakers, pathfinders. Best of all, other people feel enriched and nourished around them. Everyone they touch becomes more because they themselves *are* more. Perhaps we have needed the changes and accelerations of our time to put the flame under the crucible of becoming so that such inward alchemy could take place.

Mysticism, and spirituality in general, seems to rise during times of intense change and stress. Add the sufficiency of current shadows and the breakdown of all certainties, and we have the ingredients for the current universal pursuit of spiritual realities. We live in a time in which more and more history is happening faster and faster than we can make sense of it. The habits of millennia seem to vanish in a few months, and the convictions of centuries are crashing down like the twin towers of the World Trade Center in New York. Yet, the deconstruction of traditional ways of being may invite the underlying Spirit, of which we are a part, to break through.

So how can we birth this miracle within ourselves? How can we foster our natural birthright of spiritual presence?

Many have written of the mystical path and tracked its myriad adventures and planes of development. I have found Evelyn Underhill, writing early in the twentieth century, to be one of the finest guides to the experience. In her great work *Mysticism,* she presents the mystical path as a series of eight organic stages: awakening, purification, illumination, voices and visions, contemplation and introversion, ecstasy and rapture, the dark night of the soul, and union with the one reality.

In the first stage, awakening, one wakes up, to put it quite simply. Suddenly, the world is filled with splendor and glory, and one understands that one is a citizen in a much larger universe. One is filled with the awareness that one is a part of an enormous life, in which everything is connected to everything else.

The second stage of mystical development is called purification. Here one rids oneself of those veils and obstruction of the ordinary unexamined life that keep one from the knowledge that one has gained from awakening. One is released from old ways of being and recovers one's higher innocence. In traditional mysticism it can take the form of a very intense pursuit of asceticism. It can also take other forms of trying to create purity and beauty in the world, such as, for example, the path of Saint Francis of Assisi, who rebuilt a church as part of his purification, or of Hildegard of Bingen, who planted a garden so that God's nose might be engaged.

The traditional third stage is called the path of illumination: one is illumined in the light. The light of bliss—often experienced as actual light—literally pervades everything. One sees beauty and meaning and pattern everywhere, and yet one remains who one is and able to go about one's daily work. The stage of illumination is also one that many artists, actors, writers, visionaries, scientists, and creative people are blessed to access from time to time.

The fourth stage is called voices and visions. One sees, hears, and senses with more than five senses—an amplitude of reality including things one has never seen before, such as beings of different dimensions, angels, archetypes, numinous borderline persons, or figures from other times and realms. It is a state of revealing and interacting with a much larger reality, including those spiritual allies that lie within us.

The fifth stage is what Underhill and others call contemplation and introversion, which includes entering the silence in prayer and contemplation. It is a turning to the inner life, wherein one employs some of the vast resources of spiritual technology to journey inward to meet and receive reality in its fullness. It results in daily life as a spiritual exercise, bringing the inner and the outer lives together in a new way.

The sixth stage is referred to as ecstasy and rapture. Here the Divine Presence meets the prepared body, mind, emotions, and psyche of the mystic, which, cleared of the things that keep reality at bay, now can ecstatically receive the One. It involves the art and science of happiness.

But, alas, after all this joy and rapture, the next stage, the seventh, is what is termed the dark night of the soul, obeying the dictum that what goes up must come down. Suddenly the joy is gone, the Divine Lover is absent, God is hidden, and one is literally bereft of everything. Here one faces the remaining shadows of old forms and habits of the lesser self, preparing one to become more available to the final stage.

The eighth and last stage is called union with the one reality. Here one exists in the state of union with the one reality, experiencing the oneness Laszlo claims is the hallmark of deep spiritual experience. One is both oneself and God. For those who enter this state, it seems as if nothing is impossible; indeed, everything becomes possible. They become world changers and world servers. They become powers for life, centers for energy, partners and guides for spiritual vitality in other human beings. They glow, and they set others glowing. They are force fields, and to be in their fields is to be set glowing. They are no longer human beings as we have known them. They are fields of being, for they have moved from Godseed to Godself.

4

Extended Awareness

MICHAEL BECKWITH

There is an inner impulsion within the human being that is commonly interpreted as the engine that drives personal success, that earns credentials and accolades that result in magnificent acquisitions—the external more, more, more of which there is never enough to satisfy. For even when we have succeeded in meeting many or most of our outer goals there remains an awareness of an illusive "something," an emptiness that is yet unfilled.

Is there any validity to this awareness? Is there something woven into the fundamental fabric of our being that urges us to seek fulfillment beyond the offerings of the external world? Affirmative evidence is offered by Andrew Newberg, M.D., in his book on brain science and the biology of belief, *Why God Won't Go Away:* "As Gene and I sifted through mountains of data on religious experience, ritual, and brain science, important pieces of the puzzle came together and meaningful patterns emerged. Gradually, we shaped a hypothesis that suggests that spiritual experience, at its very root, is intimately interwoven with human biology. That biology, in some way, compels the spiritual urge."

According to both ancient and contemporary spiritual traditions, there is a passageway into an extended awareness of our true nature, that aspect of ourselves that can be accessed when the preoccupations of the conscious mind are quieted. As we enter through this passageway, we lift the veil that hides the inner paradise in which we truly live, move, and have our being. India's great philosopher Sri Aurobindo aptly describes it this way: "The full delight of being is intrinsic, self-existent, automatic; it cannot be dependent on things outside itself. In the spiritual knowledge of self, the first step is the discovery of the soul, the secret entity, the divine element within us."

From this wisdom we can conclude that there is no permanent or ultimate fulfillment from anything outside of our essential self, our soul-self. This leaves little wiggle room for us to postpone seeking out spiritual practices by which we may evolve an extended awareness of our at-one-ment with First Cause, which some call God, Brahma, Spirit, or no name at all.

Jill Bolte Taylor, a thirty-seven-year-old Harvard-trained neuroanatomist, experienced a massive stroke when a blood vessel exploded in the rational, time-oriented left side of her brain. Within a four-hour time span she lost the ability to walk, talk, read, or write. Her knowledge of how the brain works allowed her to recognize that she was having a stroke and seek immediate help. At the very outset of her eight-year recovery period, her consciousness shifted into the right brain, where she experienced a state of nirvana, what she described as an extended awareness of herself being "at one with the universe." Newberg explains this extended awareness, writing that "various key brain structures and the way information is channeled along neural pathways leads us to hypothesize that the brain possesses a neurological mechanism for self-transcendence."

To the degree in which we activate this innate capacity to self-transcend, so do we cultivate an extended awareness of the self.

As we progress in self-transcendence, the sense of separation or involvement with the personal mind expands into an awareness of the unique emanation that each of us is as an individualized expression of the One Mind that is everywhere in its fullness. That which is happening cosmically begins to happen through us locally. In such a state of awareness the plenitude, beauty, peace, joy, bliss, compassion—these transcendent yet eminent qualities of being—are activated within us. It is a process of awakening to our true nature that places us in harmony with the fundamental order of existence. Modern Zen master Huang Po describes the ultimate state of being he calls One Mind in this way: "All the Buddhas and all sentient beings are nothing but One Mind, beside which nothing exists. Only awake to the One Mind."

This One Mind is the very life force that animates and sustains existence, the evolutionary impulse within the universe and each individual.

The personal mind—predominantly the left side of the brain—wants to figure out how all of this happens. The demand to know how is actually a delaying tactic of the ego, a defense mechanism so that our sense of being a separate self doesn't dissolve right on the spot! Self-transcendence is our birthright. Everything that we need is already within us, announcing itself through the inner impulsion to grow, develop, and unfold. How do we cultivate an extended awareness of self? First by an identity shift that acknowledges our at-one-ment with the One Mind. We then grow confident in our capacity to become a fully enlightened being. As an enlightened being, we live from a state of cosmic consciousness, a conscious awareness of our oneness with all life.

When we consider current scientific studies of the brain relative to the field of quantum consciousness, the evolutionary possibilities for the individual and our global family are limitless. A genuine state of cosmic awareness expressed through an individual or a whole nation is distinguishable as scientific knowledge of life—life lived in attunement with cosmic laws. Living from such a state of consciousness holds the potential for governing our world by a kind of *superwisdom* that results in cooperation rather than competition, in unity rather than division, in oneness rather than separation.

A "Rational" Look at Spirituality

Introduction to Round Two

The second round of our discussions offers deep but entirely rational statements of the nature of spirituality and throws fresh light on the factor that could link spirituality with science: a more evolved consciousness.

Swami Kriyananda, a man who has spent a lifetime searching for truth and meaning through the spiritual experience, takes a detached view of this experience and offers an assessment of it that is clear and free of preconceptions; it could as well have come from a scientist. The difference between spirituality and science is the difference between experience based on belief and one rooted in the assessment of sensory information. Kriyananda makes a brilliant case for showing that even the pronouncements of science have an element of belief and that the doctrines and dogmas of spirituality and religion have, conversely, a basis in sensory experience. The key difference lies in science's attempt to eliminate feeling from experience and base itself purely on logic. Yet the element of feeling is part of our self-awareness, and without an awareness by the thinking subject of his or her experience no description or comprehension of experience can be full and trustworthy. In the final count, both science and spirituality are based on human experience, but on different facets of this experience. This is a profound insight that, in the search for reconciliation between these two great strands of human culture and experience, needs to be kept well in mind.

The great Indian teacher Sri Sri Ravi Shankar describes another facet of the difference between science and religion. He, too, agrees that both are based on experience, but while science explores the external world and asks, What is it?, spiritual experience is focused on the inner world and asks, Who am I? In traditional cultures these aspects of human experience are not in conflict; they complement each other. The inner-directed exploration of experience brings to the fore our intimate connection with the larger world around us—the world of nature. But in today's externally directed views the sense of this connection has been lost; no wonder that we are polluting and destroying our environment. The need is to return to the traditional practices of honoring and conserving nature, to recovering the complementarity between the outer and the inner facets of our experience. Shankar offers simple and meaningful principles that help us elevate our consciousness to achieve this paramount end.

The key to reconciling the opposition between science and spirituality is the elevation of our own consciousness so we can comprehend that the inner and outer facets of human experience are not opposed to each other, but are complementary parts of a larger whole.

Human experience is mediated by consciousness, and a better understanding of consciousness shows that both the spiritual experience and the experience of the scientist are bona fide experiences. The occurrence of spiritual experience can be grasped by the method of the sciences. The latest findings indicate that human consciousness includes elements that derive from processes of quantum resonance between perceiving subject and perceived object. British social scientist Kingsley L. Dennis cites recent experimental evidence that shows that the whole organism is a quantum-resonating nonlocal field. There is instantaneous intercommunication throughout the field, which explains the fabulous coherence of every part of the living organism with every other part as well as between this field and the fields that surround the organism—

in the final count, the whole universe. We are "entangled" with each other and with the rest of the world. This perennial insight of the spiritual teachings can now be grounded in the theories of the sciences and should encourage us to overcome the opposition between science and spirituality. Rather than dismissing each others' views, we should draw on the best insights of both spirituality and science.

Finally, Japanese scientist and software designer Shinichi Takemura discusses a surprising aspect of consciousness: the emergence of a kind of collective consciousness created by people equipped with electronic sensors. This "planetary consciousness" arises as individual humans report on conditions around them using cell phones or other devices and is enriched also by automated devices installed inter alia in automobiles. This multihuman and multitechnology system pieces together a large picture of conditions on the planet from tiny fragments, like assembling a jigsaw puzzle. The development of this global-level consciousness offers a new way for realizing an objective that is common to both science and spirituality: to sense our environment and to keep it within the limits of human well-being and livability.

5

The Real Issue

SWAMI KRIYANANDA

The real issue lies not between religion and science, but between belief and experience. Both disciplines ought to be understood in the light of man's search for *permanent* truths. Both, however—and to some extent surprisingly so—have relied too heavily on dogmas and dogmatism. In science, revolutionary scientific ideas are often laughed out of court by "the old guard"—to be accepted in time, however, after old dogmas have been replaced by new discoveries, becoming in their turn, of course, new scientific dogmas.

In one respect the difference between science and religion is noteworthy: scientific circles have yet to form bodies of hoary elders whose self-appointed role is to dictate absolutely what shall and shall not be accepted as the right beliefs. The pressure of accepted opinion, however, is almost as strong in science as in religion and acts with as much authority as any church.

For dogmatism is a phenomenon of human nature, not of human activity. The search for truth *must* move from blind belief to direct experience. Up to the present time, modern science—perhaps mainly because it was born of fresh seeking and not of oft-repeated formulae—has had the upper hand. I myself, on the other hand, am someone who began his search for truth through the sciences, but I gradually shifted my focus to the quest for God. And I have thought much about the comparative value of seeking truth outwardly, rather than inwardly. Let me add here, however, that I myself am not particularly religious. That is to say, I am not much interested in rituals intended only to propitiate God.

The first point of difference between the so-called mystical and the scientific is that logic, without feeling, can never be wholly satisfying. Logic watches, whereas *feeling* absorbs itself in the experience of what has been watched. A computer can be programmed to reason clearly, but it cannot be made to *enjoy* any of its conclusions. Nor can it be programmed to ask the deeper questions of life: the "whys." Calm feeling is not an emotion, and, instead of prejudicing reason, clarifies it. Logic can make a reasonable case for almost any argument, but only calm feeling can *know* whether that reasoning is true or false. Logic—speaking for the moment musically—can find the notes, but only feeling can arrange them in a satisfying sequence of notes, chords, and rhythms.

The materialistic sciences, in their search for abstract facts, cannot easily arrange those facts in the order of their importance to mankind. There is, moreover, another equally important difference between the mystic's and the materialist's search for truth: The materialist tries to eliminate self-awareness as prejudicial to clear judgment. The true mystic, on the other hand, tries to *clear* his sense of selfhood from prejudices by saying (I think more honestly), "Without self-awareness, where can one even begin the search for what would be interesting to anyone?"

An ice-covered lake would be difficult to break through by the application of pressure to the whole surface. By drilling at a single point, however, the ice can be penetrated easily, to reach the water underneath it. Science can indeed penetrate the coating over reality at any number of points, but without the ego-self as a point of reference, all that anyone can arrive at is a hodgepodge of irrelevant facts. It is unrealistic to try to eliminate either feeling or self-awareness from any investigation into reality. The ancient Greek saying, "Know thyself" (*"Gnothi sauton*”), remains the ultimate and highest definition of any sincere search for truth.

Scientists tend to believe that truth is infinitely complex. In this belief, there is a present-day dogma that claims that computers will someday become sophisticated enough to be self-aware. What, however, can be simpler than the common earthworm? If one touches the worm with a pin, however, the little creature will try (because it is self-aware) to squirm away, and because its awareness is centered in feeling, it will obviously *desire* to escape the pain of a pinprick.

The definition that the ancient Indian yogi-sage Patanjali gave of yoga (the supreme union of absolute understanding) was this: “*Yogas chitta vritti nirodha*” (“Yoga is the neutralization of the vortices of feeling”). A *vritti* is an eddy or whirlpool. *Chitta* has been translated—inadequately, however—as consciousness. I say “inadequately” because what the word really refers to is the *feeling* aspect of consciousness.

Science does not concentrate on feelings. It merely *explains* things. Logic alone, moreover, doesn't inspire enthusiasm for anything. Science tries to eliminate all emphasis on the self, as well as on feeling, but without self-awareness, one's efforts would lack any focus. The mystical search for truth is an inquiry into one's true place in the great scheme of things and into ways of fulfilling one's role here on Earth.

Many years ago, a man in Australia said to me, “I am an atheist. How can you explain God to me in such a way as to make me respect, or even listen to, what you are saying?”

I replied, “Why don't you try thinking of God as the highest potential you can imagine for yourself?”

For a moment the man looked taken aback. He then commented, somewhat grudgingly, “Well, yeah, I think I can live with that!”

In the context of this article, it doesn't really matter whether God exists, any more than it matters how high a mountain slope rises above any low mists hanging overhead. True mysticism seeks to climb ever upward, until endlessness is achieved. Materialistic science so far has been interested only in examining rocks on the slopes beneath us.

Whereas true mysticism is motivated by upwardly aspiring ideals, materialistic science tries, instead, to keep man satisfied with objects he sees already on the hillside.

Someday, *true* science and *true* religion together, in their desire for truth, will discover those eternal verities that alone possess the secret of unity in a single vision.

6

Our Connection to Nature

SRI SRI RAVI SHANKAR

The realities explored in science and spirituality are often assumed to be unrelated to one another. However, both find their basis in a spirit of inquiry. Modern science is objective analysis, while spirituality is subjective understanding. Science explores the outer world with a series of questions beginning with the basic query, "What is this? What is this world all about?" while spirituality begins with the question, "Who am I?"

In the ancient world these two forms of knowledge were not in conflict, but were understood to have a deep and subtle connection. Man's knowledge of himself complemented his understanding of the universe and formed the basis for a strong and healthy relationship to the creation in which he lived. It is the disconnect between these two types of knowledge that is causing many of the challenges that we face as a global community today.

Ancient wisdom describes human beings as having five layers of experience: the environment, the physical body, the mind, the intuition, and our self or spirit.

Our connection with the environment is our first level of experience and one of the most important. If our environment is clean and positive, it has a positive impact on all the other layers of our existence. As a result, they come into balance, and we experience a greater sense of peace and connection within ourselves and with others around us.

An intimate relationship with the environment is built into the human psyche. Historically, nature, mountains, rivers, trees, the sun, and the moon have always been honored in ancient cultures. It's only when we start moving away from our connection to nature and ourselves that we begin polluting and destroying the environment. We need to revive these attitudes that foster our connection with nature.

Today we live in a world where many have become greedy and want to make quick profits and achieve quick results. Their actions disrupt the ecological balance and not only pollute the physical environment, but also stimulate negative emotions on a subtle level, within themselves and also in those around them. These negative energies, expanded and compounded again and again, are the root cause of much of the violence and misery in this world.

Most wars and conflicts are triggered by such feelings and result in damage to the environment, which then takes a long time to restore and repair. We need to attend to the human psyche, which is the root cause of pollution, both physical and emotional. If compassion and care are kindled within ourselves, they will form the basis for a deeper connection to, and care for, both others and the environment.

In ancient times, if a person cut one tree, he planted five in return. The ancient people did not wash clothes in holy rivers; only ashes from cremation were submerged in the river, so that everything dissolved back into nature. We need to revive traditional practices of honoring and conserving nature.

Nature has its own means of balance. If you observe nature, you will see that the five elements that form its basis are opposed to each other. Water destroys fire, fire destroys air. Then there are so many species in nature—the birds, reptiles, mammals; all these different species are hostile toward each other, yet nature balances them out. We need to learn from nature how to balance opposing forces, within ourselves and in the world around us.

Above all, we need to be able to experience our world with an open mind that is free from stress, and from that place we need to create the means of protecting our beautiful planet Earth. For this to happen, human consciousness must rise above greed and exploitation. Spirituality, the experience of one's own nature, deep within, provides the key to this vital relationship with oneself, with others, and with our environment. This connection to our own essential nature eliminates negative emotions, elevates one's consciousness, and creates a spirit of care and commitment for the whole planet.

What would help to elevate our consciousness and deepen our connection? Here are a few basic and effective pointers:

A proper diet. Our food influences our mind. The Jain tradition has done much research on the effect of food on the mind. Ayurveda and Chinese systems and many other native systems the world over have recognized the effect of food on the psyche. Modern science confirms that food can have a direct bearing on our emotions. Emotionally disturbed children tend to eat more and suffer from obesity. A properly balanced diet has a positive impact on our emotions and thereby on our consciousness.

Light to moderate exercise. In the ancient medical system of ayurveda, there is a process of internal cleansing called *panchakarma* that involves massages, a prescribed diet, and cleansing. This has helped thousands of people to come out of stress and behavioral disorders and is also a curative for many illnesses.

Yoga, pranayama, and meditation. These are extremely vital to induce a sense of respect for one's own body and the environment. They help to maintain a toxin-free system and thereby reduce the occurrence of emotional disturbances.

Music and dance. These can bring rhythm and harmony in the body-mind complex, especially music that is not too loud and violent, music that is soothing and creates a gentle sway and rhythm in one's system, like folk and classical music.

Nature. Spending time in nature while observing silence and engaging in prayer is very congenial in regard to helping us to reflect on our own mind.

Last but not the least: service to the less fortunate.

7

Quantum Consciousness

*The Way to Reconcile
Science and Spirituality*

KINGSLEY L. DENNIS

Human thought in the twenty-first century needs to work toward a new model that immerses the human being within a vibrant, energetic universe. However, this need not demand that we throw away what we already have; rather, we can expand on the tools that have brought us to our present position. There is an Eastern proverb that roughly translates as, *"You may ride your donkey up to your front door, but would you ride it into your house?"* In other words, when we have arrived at a particular destination we are often required to make a transition in order to continue the journey. In this sense we can be grateful to a vast knowledge base of scientific and religious thought for helping us to arrive at where we presently stand. Yet, it is now imperative that we move forward. As Deepak Chopra suggested in his opening contribution to this book, how we move forward is likely to be centered in our understanding of consciousness.

Our physical apparatus is spectacular; consider that each of us carries around a 100-billion-cell bioelectric quantum computer that creates our realities, with almost all of its neurons established the day we were born. Still, this phenomenal "reality shaper" has undergone monumental perceptual change over our evolutionary history. What is required, at this significant juncture, is again another catalyst of consciousness change. This may come about through discoveries in the field of quantum biology and the idea, emphasized by Ervin Laszlo's many writings, that the form of consciousness we possess is likely to be the result of *quantum coherence.*

The human body is a constant flux of thousands of interreactions and processes connecting molecules, cells, organs, and fluids throughout the brain, body, and nervous system. Up until recently it was thought that all these countless interactions operated in a linear sequence, passing on information much like a runner passing the baton to the next runner. However, the latest findings in quantum biology and biophysics have discovered that there is in fact a tremendous degree of coherence within all living systems. It has been found through extensive scientific investigation that a form of *quantum coherence* operates within living biological systems through what are known as biological excitations and biophoton emission. What this means is that metabolic energy is stored as a form of electromechanical and electromagnetic excitations. It is these coherent excitations that are considered responsible for generating and maintaining long-range order via the transformation of energy and very weak electromagnetic signals.

After nearly twenty years of experimental research, Fritz-Albert Popp put forward the hypothesis that biophotons are emitted from a coherent electrodynamic field within the living system. What this effectively means is that each living cell is giving off, and resonating with, a biophoton field of coherent energy. If each cell is emitting this field then the whole living system is, in effect, a resonating field—a ubiquitous nonlocal field. And since it is by the means of biophotons that the living system communicates, then there is near instantaneous intercommunication throughout. And this, claims Popp, is the basis for coherent biological organization referred to as quantum coherence.

Biophysicist Mae Wan Ho has described how the living organism, including the human body, is "coherent beyond our wildest dreams" in that our bodies are constituted by a form of liquid crystal, which is an ideal transmitter of communication, resonance, and coherence. All living biological organisms continuously emit radiations of light that form a field of coherence and communication.

Moreover, biophysicists have discovered that living organisms are permeated by quantum waveforms. Ho informs us that "the visible body just happens to be where the wave function of the organism is most dense. Invisible quantum waves are spreading out from each of us and permeating into all other organisms. At the same time, each of us has the waves of every other organism entangled within our own make-up."*

This incredible new discovery actually positions each living being within a nonlocal quantum field consisting of wave interferences (where bodies meet). All people are thus not only in an emphatic relationship with each other but are also *entangled* with one another.

Neuroscience, quantum biology, and quantum physics are now beginning to converge to reveal that our bodies are not only biochemical systems but also sophisticated resonating quantum systems. These new discoveries show that a form of nonlocal connected consciousness has a physical-scientific basis. Further, it demonstrates that certain spiritual or transcendental states of collective oneness have a valid basis within the new scientific paradigm.

If we are willing to step down from the donkey we will find that our new path ahead has a place for reconciling science and spirituality. We should focus on the best of both worlds: engage in cooperation, not in conflict and competition.

---

*See Mae-Wan Ho, *The Rainbow and the Worm: The Physics of Organisms* (Singapore: World Scientific, 1998).

8
Designing a Multiperson Planetary Consciousness

SHINICHI TAKEMURA

Humankind is not the only species with the power to change the global environment. The oxygen-filled atmosphere, the moderation of the greenhouse effect, mineral resources such as limestone and oil, entire green continents—these are all created by living things. They are the result of the coevolution of billions of living organisms on Earth. Humanity's degree of influence over the environment is not exceptional in the history of this planet. What we are remarkable for is our ability to comprehensively simulate the planet's overall condition and future evolution.

At the scale of Earth, humans are tiny things, like fleas on the back of an elephant. But these tiny creatures have begun quantifying and monitoring the subtle changes in the body temperature and the physical conditions of their host, seeking ways to mitigate, or adapt to, climatic changes. Indeed, the progression of global warming and the greenhouse effect have been tracked in this way thanks to the legendary scientific observations of one tiny "flea" named Roger Keeling at the top of a Hawaiian volcano.

One unique aspect of human intelligence is its ability to apprehend conditions beyond our physical scale and see the larger picture. Today such global self-awareness is not limited to the halls of academia. In Japan, for example, grassroots weather forecasting is fast becoming a popular and effective social medium that helps avert and mitigate weather-related damage. The mobile phone site of Weathernews Inc. collects tens of thousands of weather reports daily, often with photos, by volunteer weather reporters transmitting from mobile phones.

Rapid microclimatic events such as sudden "guerrilla rain," an effect of urban heat islands, are difficult to observe and to forecast. But guided by these on-site reports (Japanese mobile phones have GPS and high-resolution cameras by which to corroborate messages with transmission times), radars can effectively detect the development of guerrilla rain clouds in near real time and send alerts to hundreds of thousands of mobile phones in the effected area thirty to sixty minutes before the guerrilla torrents fall. The current success rate in pinpoint predictions of guerrilla rain (previously impossible to forecast) is almost 80 percent, resulting in decreased damage by urbanization-related flooding.

When typhoons hit, real-time storm reports are uploaded throughout Japan. Thus citizens have self-organized into a national real-time typhoon monitoring system. By the time a storm hits Okinawa in the south, people in Tokyo, two thousand kilometers away, are in contact and report on wind and rain conditions in the capital.

These on-site reports are fully used by professionals to forecast the exact course of typhoons in order to mitigate the resulting disasters. This is a new expression of collective intelligence by "fleas" monitoring in real time the condition of the "elephant." While each flea has limited capacity for observation, when the local fragmentary information is aggregated, they create an overall picture, much like a jigsaw puzzle. (Because each individual post creates synergy with the others, I call this a "syn-active" system.)

Mobile information technologies, the jewels of modern science and technology, open new possibilities for these cocreative processes to become collective intelligence, working in situ and in real time. It is up to us to decide whether we fulfill or waste their potential. This is why it's so important that we engage our creative imagination and design "social-ware" to shape our world by each of us acting as a "global sensor," a functional part of the global neural network.

Creative social applications can repurpose automobiles to serve as nerve cells in the brains of our cities. Keio University's WIDE/LiveE! Project is using social network technologies to log cars as network devices. GPS information from hundreds of taxis not only provides real-time traffic monitoring and navigation aid to avoid traffic jams, but by mapping the condition of the cars' wipers, it also works as an additional aspect of Tokyo's networked weather information infrastructure. Brakes, too, are part of the information flow; they indicate points of increased risk of accident. Smart grid technology in the field of power generation engages consumers in interactive supply-and-demand markets, making explicit each individual's consumption as well as patterns of peak load in a community.

The evolution of automobiles and electricity into nodes in the nervous system of a participatory and attuned city can now be seen as a next step in the "intellectualization" of the global system. The image of syn-active fleas synchronizing with the dynamism of their social and global environment suggests a new relationship between humankind and the planet.

Tangible Earth, a digital globe that I have been developing since 2002, is a human interface to a sensory planetary consciousness. It was designed as a tool to empower the sensitive networking of fleas as elements in the planetary consciousness. It constantly downloads satellite data from the Internet and elsewhere and visualizes the real-time movement of weather systems, the footprint of the sun day and night, oceanic flows and seismic activities, the global migration of birds and whales, atmospheric contaminants flowing across borders, the progress of global warming, and massive real-time typhoon alerts. It's more than just a scientific data display device.

We are developing a portable version as well to be equipped with meteorological sensors and to have the same information functions as GPS-enabled mobile phones. We anticipate a time when these devices will be installed in schools and ships all over the world. These tiny global sensors will be constantly uploading real-time climate information from each location on land and sea, enabling the Tangible Earth network to become a syn-active global sensor network.

We have the power to be a cancer in the body of Earth or to be cocreators of a reflexive, ever more comprehensive living system. It's time for us to imagine and to achieve our global brain as a concrete living system—time for us to cocreate an evolution in which science and collective human consciousness embark on a common development.

Searching
for the
Meeting Ground

Introduction to Round Three

The third round of our debate discusses the possible meeting ground of science and spirituality, and the message it conveys is loud and clear. The meeting ground exists, it's under our very feet, and we just need to open our eyes to see it.

The renowned psychiatrist Stanislav Grof affirms that, as his three decades of research on the altered, so-called holotropic states of consciousness demonstrates, the experiences that make up the warp and woof of spirituality are not metaphysical and supernatural (although in themselves they are truly extraordinary): they are part of the range of human experience. And these experiences can be, and are, subjected to scientific research. There is no opposition between science and spirituality when it comes to the experiences that ground spirituality; the opposition comes into play only when spirituality is allowed to degenerate into religious dogma for purposes of control and power in society.

The equally renowned medical doctor Larry Dossey, perhaps the foremost pioneer of "nonlocal medicine," shows that the powers of our brain and consciousness include the power to heal—to heal over any distance, and not by physical or chemical means, but through the subtle but often more effective transmission of information. Despite criticism and even downright rejection by the conservative mainstream of the medical establishment, the acceptance of the role of spirituality in medicine is actually under way. Here, too, the insight that emerges is that spirituality and science are not incompatible. On the contrary, an open and comprehensive approach in science recognizes spirituality as a definite factor in the timeless enterprise of healing the human body—and mind—of the diseases that occasionally beset it.

Next, the great visionary Barbara Marx Hubbard writes that the union of science and spirituality will come about in the course of the next evolutionary development of the human species. The integration of science, technology, and spirituality is already happening—not by chance, but because it has become a survival imperative of our species.

To end our round three, famed Dutch Rabbi Awraham Soetendorp presents a testimony that comes from the ranks of the great world religions. In the parable of the Jewish people he cites, the original light that assisted God in creating the universe and the human being had escaped; the vessels in which it was contained were torn apart, and all creation was threatened to fall asunder. This was reflected in the historic exile of the Jewish people. Today the time has come to join together to muster the spiritual and physical energies to heal ourselves and Earth. The rays of light will be retrieved when the whisper of truth shared by science and spirituality is amplified; then the broken vessels that contained the light will be whole again.

These contributions, by two scientists and two persons of great spirituality, make it quite clear: in these times of grave danger as well as unparalleled evolutionary opportunity, finding common ground between science and spirituality is a crucial challenge awaiting both communities.

9

Science and Spirituality

*Observations from
Modern Consciousness Research*

STANISLAV GROF

The leading philosophy of Western science has been monistic material-ism. Various scientific disciplines have described the history of the universe as the history of developing matter and accept as real only what can be measured and weighed. Life, consciousness, and intelligence are seen as more or less accidental side products of material processes. Physicists, biologists, and chemists recognize the existence of dimensions of reality that are not accessible to our senses, but only those that are physical in nature and can be revealed and explored with the use of various extensions of our senses, such as microscopes or telescopes, specially designed recording devices, and laboratory experiments.

In a universe understood this way, there is no place for spirituality of any kind. The existence of God, the idea that there are invisible dimensions of reality inhabited by nonmaterial beings, the possibility of the survival of consciousness after death, and the concepts of reincarnation and karma have been relegated to fairy tales and handbooks of psychiatry. From a psychiatric perspective to take such things seriously means to be ignorant, unfamiliar with the discoveries of science, superstitious, and subject to primitive magical thinking. If the belief in God or Goddess occurs in intelligent persons, it is seen as an indication that they have not come to terms with infantile images of their parents as omnipotent beings they had created in their infancy and childhood. And direct experiences of spiritual realities are considered manifestations of serious mental diseases—psychoses.

The study of holotropic states has thrown new light on the problem of spirituality and religion. The key to this new understanding is the discovery that in these states it is possible to encounter a rich array of experiences that are very similar to those that inspired the great religions of the world—visions of God and various divine and demonic beings, encounters with discarnate entities, episodes of psychospiritual death and rebirth, visits to heaven and hell, past-life experiences, and many others. Modern research has shown beyond any doubt that these experiences are not products of pathological processes afflicting the brain, but manifestations of archetypal material from the collective unconscious, and thus normal and essential constituents of the human psyche. Although these mythical elements are accessed intrapsychically in a process of experiential self-exploration and introspection, they are ontologically real and have objective existence.

In view of these observations, the fierce battle that religion and science have fought over the last few centuries appears ludicrous and completely unnecessary. Genuine science and authentic religion do not compete for the same territory; they represent two approaches to existence that are complementary, not competitive. Science studies phenomena in the material world, the realm of the measurable and weighable; spirituality and true religion draw their inspiration from experiential knowledge of the aspect of the world that Jungians refer to as "imaginal" to distinguish it from imaginary products of individual fantasy or psychopathology. This imaginal world manifests in what I call "holotropic states of consciousness," the altered states in which those religion-inspiring experiences surface. Modern research has shown that these are not products of pathological processes afflicting the brain, but manifestations of archetypal material from the collective unconscious, and thus normal and essential constituents of the human psyche. The matrices for them exist in deep recesses of the unconscious psyche of every human being.

Spirituality is a very important and natural dimension of the human psyche, and the spiritual quest is a legitimate and fully justified human endeavor. However, it is necessary to emphasize that this applies to genuine spirituality based on personal experience and does not provide support for ideologies and dogmas of organized religions. To prevent misunderstanding and confusion that in the past compromised many similar discussions, it is critical to make a clear distinction between spirituality and religion.

Spirituality is based on direct experiences of ordinarily invisible numinous dimensions of reality, which become available in holotropic states of consciousness. It does not require a special place or officially appointed persons mediating contact with the divine. The mystics do not need churches or temples. The context in which they experience the sacred dimensions of reality, including their own divinity, is provided by their bodies and nature. And instead of officiating priests, they need a supportive group of fellow seekers or the guidance of a teacher who is more advanced on the inner journey than they are themselves.

Organized religions tend to create hierarchical systems focusing on the pursuit of power, control, politics, money, possessions, and other worldly concerns. Under these circumstances, religious hierarchy as a rule dislikes and discourages direct spiritual experiences in its members because they foster independence and the members cannot be effectively controlled. When this is the case, genuine spiritual life continues only in the mystical branches, monastic orders, and ecstatic sects of the religions involved. A deep mystical experience tends to dissolve the boundaries between religions and reveals deep connections between them, while the dogmatism of organized religions tends to emphasize differences between various creeds and engenders antagonism and hostility.

There is no doubt that the dogmas of organized religions are generally in fundamental conflict with science, whether this science uses the mechanistic-materialistic model or is anchored in the emerging paradigm. However, the situation is very different in regard to authentic mysticism based on spiritual experiences. The great mystical traditions have amassed extensive knowledge about human consciousness and about the spiritual realms in a way that is similar to the method that scientists use in acquiring knowledge about the material world. It involves a methodology for inducing transpersonal experiences, systematic collection of data, and intersubjective validation. Spiritual experiences, like any other aspect of reality, can be subjected to careful open-minded research and studied scientifically.

Scientifically conducted consciousness research has brought convincing evidence for the objective existence of the imaginal realm and has thus validated the main metaphysical assumptions of the mystical worldview, the Eastern spiritual philosophies, and even certain beliefs of native cultures.

The conflict between religion and science reflects a fundamental misunderstanding of both. As Ken Wilber has pointed out, there cannot be a conflict between science and religion if both these fields are properly understood and practiced. If there seems to be a conflict, we are likely dealing with "bogus science" and "bogus religion." The apparent incompatibility is due to the fact that either side seriously misunderstands the other's position and very likely represents also a false version of its own discipline.

10

Spirituality, Healing, and Science

LARRY DOSSEY

What is spirituality? I consider it a felt sense of connectedness with *something higher,* a presence that transcends the individual sense of self. I distinguish spirituality from religion, which is a codified system of beliefs, practices, and behaviors that usually take place in a community of like-minded believers. Religion may or may not include a sense of the spiritual, and spiritual individuals may or may not be religious. I regard prayer as communication with the Absolute, however named, no matter what form this communication may take. Prayer may or may not be addressed to a Supreme Being. Many forms of Buddhism, for instance, are not theistic, yet prayer, addressed to the universe, is a vital part of the Buddhist tradition.

Even if prayer connects us with the Absolute, does it work in an empirical sense? In regard to healing, many systematic and meta-analyses have been published in the peer-reviewed medical literature assessing the quality of remote healing and distant intentionality studies. Nearly all these peer-reviewed analyses have yielded positive findings, suggesting that the healing effects of prayer and other forms of intentionality are real and replicable.

Yet these studies evoke sharp criticism. It is an article of faith in most scientific circles that human consciousness is derived from the brain and that its effects are confined to the brain and body of an individual. Accordingly, it is widely assumed that conscious intentions cannot act remotely. The controlled healing studies call this assumption into question, and this challenge, I suspect, underlies much of the visceral response this field evokes.

Perhaps the most frequent criticism of distant-intentionality-and-healing studies is that they are so theoretically implausible that they should not even be done. In other words, they radically violate the accepted canons of science, and this places them so completely outside the scientific landscape that they do not deserve consideration.

There are striking parallels between the current rejection of distant healing phenomena and the earlier refusal of scientists to accept the phenomenon of meteorites. The *logic* in both instances is that because scientists know in advance that certain events can't happen, they don't happen.

Plausibility arguments can especially become a straightjacket in areas in which current understanding is primitive. Nowhere is this truer than in areas in which the operations of consciousness are concerned. For example, physicist Sir Roger Penrose states, "My position [on consciousness] demands a major revolution in physics. . . . I've come to believe that there is something very fundamental missing from current science. . . . Our understanding at this time is not adequate and we're going to have to move to new regions of science."

Many outstanding scientists do not believe that remote effects of consciousness, if they occur, are implausible with respect to current scientific theory. For example, physicist Gerald Feinberg states, "If such phenomena indeed occur, no change in the fundamental equations of physics would be needed to describe them."

As physicist O. Costa de Beauregard observes, "Today's physics allows for the existence of the so-called 'paranormal' phenomena of telepathy, precognition, and psychokinesis. . . . The whole concept of 'non-locality' in contemporary physics requires this possibility."

Henry P. Stapp of the University of California–Berkeley states, "Our human thoughts are linked to nature by nonlocal connections: what a person chooses to do in one region seems immediately to effect what is true elsewhere in the universe. . . . [Our] thoughts . . . DO something." (emphasis in original)

These positions do not endorse remote healing through distant intentionality, of course, but they appear to leave open the possibility.

Another common criticism is that these studies are metaphysical, that they invoke a transcendent agency or higher power, which places them outside the domain of empirical science. This is a straw-man argument because researchers in this field make no assertions about entelechies, gods, or metaphysical agents in interpreting their findings. They are searching for correlations between healing intentions and observable effects in the world. They typically defer on the question of mechanism, which is an accepted strategy within science.

Researchers are currently exploring hypotheses from several areas of science that are cordial to the remote effects of prayer and intentionality. Indeed, the acceptance of a role for spirituality in modern medicine is well underway, and for good reason. Compelling evidence suggests that those who follow a spiritual path in their life live several years longer than those who do not follow such a path and that they experience a lower incidence of almost all major diseases.

During my medical training I was assured that *real doctors* don't believe in a role for spirituality in healing. Prayer was especially derided as unscientific nonsense. I doubt that these prejudices ever truly reflected the inner beliefs of most physicians. In any case, they certainly do not do so today. A recent nationwide survey of American physicians in various subspecialties found that 59 percent pray for their patients individually, 51 percent pray for their patients as a group, 42 percent encourage their patients to pray for themselves, and 55 percent say they have seen clinical events among their patients that they consider miraculous.

A survey of American family physicians found that 99 percent are convinced that spiritual beliefs can heal and 75 percent believe that prayers of others can help a patient recover. The Joint Commission, which accredits clinics and hospitals in the United States, requires every institution to have a method in place to assess the spiritual concerns of every incoming patient. The Association of American Medical Colleges requires that every graduating physician be able to take a spiritual history from a patient, demonstrate that he or she understands how spirituality can be used to deliver compassionate care to those in need, and demonstrate a knowledge of the research on the role of spirituality in health. A recent survey of over four thousand nurses found that 80 percent felt that spirituality should be covered in nursing education as a core aspect of nursing.

I am not recommending a mindless homogenization of religion and scientific medicine, which would be disastrous, but that we simply acknowledge the fact, now demonstrated in hundreds of studies, that spiritual concerns and healing intentions influence clinical outcomes and longevity. This research is abundant and is increasing. To ignore it is, I believe, scientifically untenable.

Yet this field will continue to evoke intellectual indigestion. Those who consider spirituality and healing intentions outside the purview of scientific medicine may ignore them. In doing so, however, critics should be careful not to obstruct free inquiry and subvert the very science they champion. Those who consider distant intentionality and remote healing so implausible they simply cannot countenance the generous evidence favoring them might consider the observation of William James: "I believe there is no source of deception in the investigation of nature which can compare with a fixed belief that certain kinds of phenomena are *impossible.*"

11

Conscious Evolution as a Context for the Integration of Science and Spirituality

BARBARA MARX HUBBARD

We are today living not only through a crisis that could destroy civilization and our essential life-support systems, but also through a deeper phase-change in evolution itself. We are entering the first age of conscious evolution—the evolution of evolution itself, from unconsciousness to a conscious choice.

This phase-change began noticeably and violently when the United States dropped the first atomic bombs on Japan in 1945. A signal went through the social body that we now have the power to destroy our world; self-centered consciousness with this degree of power is not viable in the long run.

We are the first species who faces extinction by its own acts and knows it.

This is just the beginning. Through the advent of evolutionary technologies such as biotechnology, nano-technology, robotics, space travel, the quest for zero point energy devices, and more, the human species is gaining powers it had previously attributed only to gods.

But not only can we destroy our own life-support systems, we can also catch a glimmer of our potential for a radical transformation of an evolutionary order.

When we imagine ourselves going through this crisis, hard as it may be, and project ourselves forward into the more distant future, even a mere one hundred years, we see the emergence of a "universal species" capable of coevolving with nature and cocreating with spirit. We learn to be in alignment with the drive in nature toward complexity and consciousness—on this Earth, in our solar system, and eventually in the galaxies beyond.

Out of our many emergencies is coming emergence, and out of competition a greater cooperation as social networking escalates among those who are innovating and transforming. We appear on the threshold of a nonlinear, exponential connectivity that is highly creative.

The integration of science, spirituality, and technology is happening.

One of the great advances of science itself has been the relatively recent discovery of cosmogenesis, the universe story, as Brian Swimme and Thomas Berry call it—*the mysterious, indeed awesome awareness that out of no thing at all has evolved everything that was, that is, and will be.* We are participants in an evolutionary drama, our own birth narrative. We are becoming the universe in person!

The *mystery of the process of creation* is beyond human understanding, yet we note through science many recurring patterns. We see how nature has evolved, crisis after crisis, toward higher consciousness, complexity, and order for billion of years, often pressed forward by the crises themselves.

Our new, scientifically based, evolutionary universe story has given us the insight that nature and we ourselves are evolving. There is a direction in this process toward more complex order, more awareness, and more freedom to destroy or to evolve.

Many of us are working together toward something we have never seen on any scale before—a sustainable, evolvable, cocreative society in which each person is encouraged to do and be his or her best. A global mind/heart of coherence and love is arising in the midst of fear, competition, and chaos.

An evolutionary spirituality is emerging, experienced as the *impulse of evolution,* the *process of creation,* the *implicate order,* a patterning process coming through our own hearts. It is felt as the sacred core of the evolutionary spiral, as the evolving godhead arising or even incarnating within each of us as our own impulse to cocreate. It is the "creator within" expressing itself uniquely through each person as a new form of "social cosmogenesis." The generating power of universal evolution is guiding us toward a more synergistic, cooperative democracy.

Through the natural evolution of complexity and consciousness, driven by mounting advances in communication, connectivity, and spiritual practices, millions of us are gaining the experience of being connected with *the field out of which everything is coarising,* internalized as inner guidance, the quiet voice of God.

It is as though we're undergoing the evolution of our species not as extraordinary beings, but as the *new norm.* Great avatars, saints, and mystics had paved the way. Pioneering souls of the twenty-first century are exploring how to become creators, coevolvers, universal humans.

This emerging human has been called by many names. Teilhard de Chardin called it *the ultra human,* or *Homo progressivus,* in whom the "flame of expectation burns, attracted toward the future as an organism progressing toward the unknown." Sri Aurobindo, the great Indian evolutionary sage, called this the *gnostic human,* the individual in whom the Consciousness Force itself, the supramental power of universal creativity, incarnates and begins to transform the body/mind into the very cells that evolve beyond the human phase.

Others have called this *Homo noeticus,* a being of gnosis or deep knowing of the field out of which we are coarising. Or *Homo divina,* as Sister Judy Cauley puts it. Or the universal human, connected through the heart to the whole of life, awakening from within by the *core of the spiral of evolution.* The implicate order is becoming explicate in us, turning into the essential self, animated by a passionate life purpose to express our creativity.

There is no reason to assume that the evolution of humanity stops with today's form of *Homo sapiens sapiens.* We are obviously a young species, immature, incomplete, and actually not viable in our current state of consciousness. The ultimate hope, I believe, is that the evolution of consciousness and freedom is occurring naturally within millions of us, as a sort of *spontaneous evolution,* an inner *punctuated equilibrium* amidst the chaos, and that we are realizing that as the offspring of the universal evolution we are integral parts of nature and that the evolutionary process is happening within us when we open our eyes to see it, and be it, and do our best to participate in it.

As spirituality, science, and technology blend, the evolutionary story becomes in us the *sacred way of conscious evolution*—a developmental path toward the coevolution of a universal humanity.

12

Retrieving the
Hidden Rays of Light
A Global Partnership Is Emerging

RABBI AWRAHAM SOETENDORP

In the heart of the Jewish mystical tradition there is the parable of primordial light and the creation out of nothingness, *en sof*

> At the beginning of creation Gd spoke, Jehi Or let there be light
> This refers to the primordial light that assisted Him in creating the
> universe and its fullness
> When the inner decision was made to create the human being with
> his and her ability to choose, *lehavdil*
> To differentiate between good and bad, the holy and the profane He
> needed as it were to silence this light
> which had been created before the sun the moon and the stars were
> fashioned
> Gd therefore assembled this light and put it in casks
> He then proceeded to breathe in, *Tsimtsum,* to be completely absent
> even for the smallest moment
> In order to allow space to exist in which the human could develop

her Gd-like essence independently

As expressed in the Divine intention

Let Us create Adam according to Our Image

Utter darkness reigned and tore with unending force at the just created human frame

And broke the vessels

All creation threatened to fall asunder

And Gd breathed out again and filled the universe again with His splendor

In that smallest entity of time when darkness was complete and all creation ran the risk of returning to Chaos again

The human being was formed in its fullest potential

The rays of light which escaped from the broken vessels seemed however to be lost forever

But now the fusion between the Divine intention and the newly created human potential came into being

The human is able and thus commanded to retrieve the wandering rays of light, which came entangled into

The most unlikely hidden corners of existence by the performing of mitzvot deeds of kindness

By being human in the most inhuman circumstances

Thus the banishment of Jews to all the corners of the Earth is a blessing in disguise

Jews are able to encounter the rays of light everywhere

Every time a ray is discovered through deeds of kindness it returns immediately to its original source of being

And when thus all rays have been retrieved the Messianic time of peace and righteousness is upon us.

This parable had a particular, powerful, and comforting influence during the long, ever recurring period of exile the Jewish people had endured. In our time its power has not diminished; on the contrary, it now allows all human beings an insight into the fabric of existence where the physical and the spiritual are intertwined and to act upon it. Gershom Sholem, the greatest searcher into the depths of Jewish mysticism, ventured the question at the end of his life: What will be the new parable, which will express our bewilderment after the Shoa and the new reality of a world threatened by extinction?

Holistic concepts have arisen in recent years, such as the Earth Charter, the Charter for Compassion, and the Universal Statement on Spirituality, in which the golden rule is the binding principle. Ecological integrity, care, and respect for the whole community of life, social and economic justice, democracy, nonviolence, and peace are rightfully seen as bound together. In the symbolic figure of Adam Kadmon, the primordial man, mystics have attempted to show the interconnectedness of the physical and spiritual realms.

The translation into responsible living as world citizens is alluded to in the images used in various traditions. The world community is one body. When one part of the body aches the rest of the body feels the pain. The moment this does not occur the beginning of death sets in. The technological advances in the field of communication have only enhanced this consciousness. This has always been part of the human condition. Ever since the human was banished from the Garden of Eden, the golden cage, we have been challenged to repair the world, the *tikkun olam,* thereby restoring creation to its divinely intended meaning.

My father of blessed memory defined this ultimate purpose in a letter to a young friend who was in hiding during the German occupation of the Netherlands as a world filled with cooperation, love, truth, and righteousness. *Olam,* the Hebrew word for universe, has a double meaning: infinite time and boundless space. The essence is interaction.

In the words of the Earth Charter, we stand at a critical moment in Earth's history, a time when humanity must choose its future. The choice is ours: form a global partnership to care for Earth and for each other, or risk destroying ourselves.

In the biblical account, right after the flood the surviving community achieved the goal of unified action. They used it to build the

Tower of Babel. Their mistake was not that they tried to make a name for themselves, but that the process of building was misguided. Stones became more important than people. When a human being fell, he or she could be replaced by the next on the ladder. But when a stone fell, it had to be carried up all the way from the bottom. The opportunity to foster a global partnership was squandered, and humanity was dispersed all over Earth, with no understanding among them anymore. Ours is the time to attempt again to collect the physical and the spiritual energies within infinite space and infinite time to be fused together.

All is in the hands of Gd except the reverence for him. Our choice in this moment of utter forlornness will change the form and the content of the universe. We are truly living the birth pains of the messianic time. The rays of light will be retrieved when the whisper of truth that science and spirituality share is amplified and the broken vessels are healed.

Stepping-Stones toward Unification

Introduction to Round Four

Round Four of the book both widens and deepens the ground covered in the previous three rounds.

Hiroshi Tasaka, the Japanese poet-scientist—a distinguished economist in his own right—affirms that, in the dialectical process championed already by Georg Hegel, opposites fuse in a higher union. This will be the fate also of science and spirituality: opposites today, yet fused in a higher union tomorrow. In order to help this process (as Hegel would have called it, to be the midwife of its historical dialectic) Tasaka advocates three distinct but complementary strategies. The first concerns natural science and points to the nearly miraculous facts discovered by cosmology as a way to inspire a truly spiritual sense of wonder. The second regards the science of psychology and calls on psychologists to draw on the wisdom of centuries developed in the spiritual traditions to complement the scientific search for the comprehension of such phenomena as, for instance, "the collective subconscious." The third strategy is for social scientists to combine the manifestations of the Internet revolution with their own economic science and move into the twenty-first century, beyond the classical doctrines toward a more humane "compassion capitalism."

The cross-fertilization of cutting-edge science and traditional

spirituality is also the subject of the visionary and deeply spiritual—
yet eminently rational—contribution of James O'Dea. He highlights
the facile and entirely mistaken tendency of some observers to leap to
metaphysical and/or theological conclusions in considering the staggering findings of high-energy physics. Can the data from a supercollider
throw light on the existence (or nonexistence) of God? Neither Plato
nor David Bohm would have agreed. The problem remains to overcome
the inherent reductionism of the narrow interpretation of scientific
findings and find the way to reconcile it with the experience of being in
a living universe. There are ways of knowing that open profound states
of unity and ecstatic awareness far beyond the ken of science. All the
more reason, perhaps, for trying to facilitate the dialectical fusion of
science and spirituality advocated by Tasaka.

The next contribution to this round comes from one of the most
noted visionary-scientists of our time: the anthropologist and noosphere researcher José Argüelles. In his view the noosphere is that
state of transformed order in the affairs of humanity that constitutes
the necessary stepping-stone to a radically new world—a new civilization with a different consciousness. For Argüelles it is the discipline
of "geoesthetics"—a planetary science-art—that is called on to transform Earth into a work of art, establishing our connection with the
universe.

Where do all these wide-ranging explorations really meet? The
well-known journalist and Internet blogger Alison Rose Levy gives
an answer: they meet in the curiosity that underlies all inquiry into
nature and experience, whether in the spiritual or in the scientific
domain. She invites us to shed every shadow of dogmatism, whether
in religion or in science, to overcome everything that would limit the
ranging of our deep curiosity over the terrains that we are to explore.
We need to bring together the inner and the outer dimensions of our
existence and experience—the spiritual and the scientific—and range
throughout the experiential and existential domains of the personal,
the interpersonal, and the collective.

In this round, the same as in the previous rounds, no easy answers are given. But a consensus comes gradually to light: today we live in two worlds, in two cultures. Finding the way to connect them, and ultimately to fuse them, is an unsolved challenge. But it is one that we need to perceive and to accept, for the meeting of science and spirituality remains one of the fundamental preconditions of our life and well-being—and even of our survival on this mindlessly ravaged and deeply disoriented planet.

13

Three Strategies to Promote the Fusion of Science and Spirituality

HIROSHI TASAKA

What is the most important thing that will happen in the twenty-first century?

The fusion of science and spirituality.

That will happen.

Why will this happen?

Because this world in which we live changes, develops, progresses, and evolves according to a certain law: the law of interpenetration of the dialectic.

This law was advocated by Georg Hegel, a German philosopher.

And this law teaches us that "things which oppose and compete with each other come to resemble each other."

If this Hegelian law is correct, science and spirituality will come to resemble each other, merge with each other, and fuse into a higher and greater "something."

Then, two questions arise in our minds:

How will this fusion happen?

And how can we promote this fusion?

The latter is especially of great importance in the twenty-first century because now, at the beginning of this century, both science and spirituality are faced with their limitations.

So I would like to propose here "strategies" to promote the fusion of science and spirituality.

THE FIRST STRATEGY: FOR NATURAL SCIENCE

Teaching Modern Science in the Religious Community

When we learn the latest findings in the forefront of modern science, the so-called "sense of wonder" naturally comes to our mind.

For instance, according to the latest scientific knowledge, this universe was created from a "quantum vacuum" 13.7 billion years ago.

At the beginning, the quantum vacuum created a countless number of bubbles that are called "baby universes."

And most of the baby universes disappeared shortly after their birth.

But among those countless baby universes, the universe in which we live has miraculously survived.

A sense of wonder naturally comes to our minds when we learn this scientific fact about the creation of the universe.

And this sense of wonder is indispensable for a religious mind and spirituality.

Therefore, teaching the latest science is one of the best ways for people to gain a religious mind and spirituality in today's world.

THE SECOND STRATEGY:
FOR HUMAN SCIENCE

Deepening Modern Psychology through the Wisdom
of Traditional Religions and Spirituality

The most important question for the science of psychology in the twenty-first century is, Who am I?

To answer this profound question, we need to explore the depths of our mind, especially the world of the subconsciousness advocated by Sigmund Freud and the world of the collective subconsciousness advocated by Carl Gustav Jung.

But the wisdom of traditional religions and spirituality has already been exploring such worlds for the past several thousand years.

For instance, Buddhism has been exploring the world of the collective subconscious through the notions of *manas-vijñāna* (the seventh consciousness) and *ālaya-vijñāna* (the eighth consciousness) for several thousand years.

So, we need to deepen modern psychology through the vast wisdom of traditional religions and spirituality fostered throughout their long history.

Then, one important question arises in our minds, Where can we find and observe the world of the collective subconscious?

In the Internet communities.

If we look into the Internet communities, we can see and feel the world of the collective subconscious of people.

Also, in the Internet communities, we can express different aspects of ourselves, multipersonalities, by using avatars or being anonymous.

And this is one good way to find the answer to the deep question, Who am I?

THE THIRD STRATEGY:
FOR SOCIAL SCIENCE

Creating a New Economic Principle by Combining the
Internet Revolution and the Wisdom of Compassion
in Traditional Religions and Spirituality

Modern capitalism has been based on a monetary economy, which refers to the economic activities of people motivated by acquiring money.

That is the reason why modern capitalism tends to stimulate the greedy mind of people and tends to become so-called "greedy capitalism."

But the Internet revolution that started in 1995 has been reviving an old economic principle called a gift economy or a voluntary economy, which refers to the economic activities of people motivated by "satisfying the mind," for instance, and by affection and compassion for other people.

So, if we combine the Internet revolution, modern economic science, and the wisdom of compassion in traditional religions and spirituality, we will be able to create "compassion capitalism" in the twenty-first century.

These are the three strategies I propose in order to promote the fusion of science and spirituality. And this is not just a vision or strategies for the future; this is a movement that is already starting to happen in the world.

14

Finding the Holy of Holies

Sticky Particles and the Ground of All Being

JAMES O'DEA

There was some excitement at the Tevatron collider site in the United States recently, not because they had found what has been mischievously referred to as the "God particle," but because they had ruled out a quarter of the energy range where the Higgs particle is said to exist. Meanwhile the contest of the colliders is still on, with researchers at the Large Hadron Collider in Switzerland reasonably confident that they will be in a position to be much more definitive about the all important particle sometime in 2013.

The Higgs particle is so important because, if found, it would resolve the great mystery that clouds our understanding as to how energy gains mass on the way to becoming matter. It has been described as the molasses that acts as the sticky stuff in the universe, serving the formation of matter's atomic building blocks.

Could it be that materialists are waiting to say that the Higgs particle will now replace God? Or that more people will turn to atheism at the realization that God is not sitting there as an instrumental agent who turns invisible forces into stars and planets? Having declared that the hand of God is really a sticky particle, it will be one more nail in the coffin of the Creator and one more challenge to the idea that consciousness is the first cause, primary field, or ground of being out of which everything arises!

"Well not so fast," says Plato. In his own way he saw this coming. In his day, he complained that some of the philosophers were beginning to surmise that the universe was chiefly composed of rocks and gases. He reminded them that the universe has not only measurable quantities, but it also has qualities. These qualities were the progenitors of form: truth, beauty, love, justice, harmony—all these qualities combined in different degrees to give birth to ideas and to interfuse and give life to diverse forms.

I was recently at the annual *Language of Spirit* dialogue, which was instigated eighteen years ago by the physicist David Bohm and his Native American counterpart Leroy Little Bear. We are all familiar with the native sense of "all my relations," and by that they mean the relatedness of every form in existence. What struck me at this last dialogue was how much the native elders stressed *being known by place*. They quipped that Westerners are always on the move and moving into other people's territories because they never stay long enough to know and be known by place. I found it a startling idea that I could enter a relationship with place to the degree that it becomes a field of mutual appreciation: maybe that finch on the tree and I could commune rather than its being simply admired by me; perhaps even the qualities in the tree itself could mentor me, or the rocks, stones, and crystals could reflect qualities beyond the spectacular geometry of their formation. Is all life looking at itself and its relatives as a reflection in a mirror we call consciousness?

Bohm was so interested in dialogue because it helped open us up to the deep mirror of consciousness itself. He saw the manifest aspect of the universe in space and time as part of an explicate order, but also saw that underlying the substrate of matter is an implicate order, which is generative and holographic. He suggests there is a "proto-intelligence" in matter since it arises out of an implicate order that is a seedbed of consciousness. He says, "The separation of the two, matter and spirit, is an abstraction."

Meanwhile the colliders are busy searching the energy range, measured in gigaelectronvolts, where the holy of holies, in the realm of physics, may have hidden itself. And even if they manage to nab it, what will it really mean for those of us who believe that as long as spirit is denied science will continue to live its current schizophrenia as both *evocateur* of human possibilities and enlightenment and servant of a frighteningly reductionist materialism.

What will it mean? It will mean the difference between whether we see ourselves in a living universe or one designed for machines, for consumption and competition over ever increasingly limited resources. It will mean the difference between continued rebellion against the holy order of nature or the reemergence of nature as our greatest teacher. It will mean the difference between biophilia and necrophilia, that is, love of life or love of dead things. Loving your right to a gas-guzzling car over protection of the ecosphere is a form of necrophilia. It goes with a consume, junk, and dump approach because, anyway, it's all dead stuff. With such necrophilia comes the loss of one-third of Earth's species since 1970 and looming ecological and climate-related catastrophes.

But the lovers of life look for the remarriage of science and spirituality, where we explore the ground of all being, seek to know it better, appreciate the many ways to understand it, and come in some humility to feed from a holy of holies that resides inside the great mystery. Such knowing opens us to profound states of unity and ecstatic awareness, which no sticky little particle, however brilliant, is capable of delivering on its own.

15

Geoesthetics

The Spiritualization of Art and Science in the Noosphere

JOSÉ ARGÜELLES

A reversal of world values, a spiritual concept of the Earth as God-created and sacred, is in order before we two leggeds can be environmentally effective on a global basis.

ED MCGAA, *MOTHER EARTH SPIRITUALITY*

The acceleration of Earth changes as we approach 2012 is intimately connected to the fact that we live in a prevailing worldview that is anything but sacred. A sacred worldview is one that views things as a whole, where every part or detail of nature in some way is a manifestation of a divine presence or a divine law. In such a worldview respect for all that exists is the supreme guiding principle.

The rape of nature, the degradation of the biosphere, and the deterioration of the social and moral values of the predominant global civilization can all be attributed to the loss of our sacred view. Instead of a wholeness—holiness—of vision, there is a separation, a secular divisiveness that propagates itself into ever more finite, analytical bits of information, until we arrive at the present situation, where, decapitated of a hierarchy of values, chaos and anarchy reign in every aspect of human endeavor. Not the least of this atomization of the whole is the rise and dominance of the individual ego, aided and exacerbated by the ultimate cybertechnologies of social networking.

The rise of secular, materialist science since the seventeenth century has been the principle factor and driving force underlying this state of affairs. In establishing a thoroughly profane worldview and world order, modern science is also at the root of the consumer-oriented society of profligate values and profound disconnection from nature, resulting in a disordering of the sacred whole.

If modern science is the engine driving the creation of a sacred disorder that is planetary in scope, art is its reflective medium. Since the scientific revolution the course of art has spiraled into its own devolution of disassociation and devaluation of any clear, socially coherent vision. Modernist and postmodernist art side by side with a pop culture that, for the most part, relentlessly descends into ever greater depths of vulgarity, vividly mirror the schizophrenic loss of the sacred view.

This degeneration of values owes much to the notion that art and science are separate disciplines and value systems. In a whole system or sacred view this is not the case; science as knowing and art as doing are mutually interactive.

As we approach the climactic end point of December 21, 2012, it is clear that the evolutionary pendulum is swinging. The reversal of world values toward a spiritual concept of Earth as God-created and sacred is inevitable. There is a dialectic higher than that of materialism—a cosmic evolutionary dialectic that operates by principles of self-transcendence.

When an organism reaches a state of irreducible complexity and whole-system crisis, in order to survive it advances to a new level of simplicity and experiences a radical reorganization of its functions to encompass an expanded worldview. In the evolutionary cycle of the planet of which we are integral members, this new order is referred to as the noosphere—the great awakening of mind and spirit that beckons for the other side of 2012.

The momentousness of the noospheric shift cannot be underestimated. It is the greatest event in Earth's history since the transition from matter to life 500 million years ago. Now life gives way to the world of mind. Life is but the intermediate term between matter and mind. As Earth once evolved from the Proterozoic to Paleozoic eras, it now advances from the Cenozoic to the Psychozoic—the noosphere, the unified mind of Earth, and the consequent spiritualization of life and matter.

This magnificent mutational shift will advance our perceptions into a whole and sacred way once again. This whole-order perception is the natural condition of the universal mind. Cosmos proceeds from the Universal One, the source of sacred being, the breath of the universe, endowing everything with a sacred wholeness, from the atoms to the human beings, the two-legged entities treading on Earth. And as everything is interconnected, the human is but an expression of Earth, the bearer and transmitter of Earth's mind, the noosphere.

The universe never stopped being sacred; it is only humanity that lost its sacred view. Restored to intrinsic wholeness, the noospheric human will discover that art is the principle medium of the evolution of consciousness throughout the cosmos and that underlying this artistic intent is a sacred science that proceeds from the whole to embrace the multidimensional universe by a single unifying law.

As the perceptual organs of Earth, humans will innately operate with a sacred view. We will not separate and divide as we once did, but will realize reality as sets of mutually complementary functions within a whole—the sacred round. We will understand quite simply that art is how we do things and science is how we know things. We cannot do something properly without a way of knowing, while knowing without doing is useless. All knowing is of a whole system; all doing advances the order of the whole.

The consequence of the emerging consciousness of the noosphere will be the spiritualization of art and science as well as their fusion into a new quality of perception: *geoesthesis,* the intrinsic perception that the

Earthly environment as a whole is organized according to cosmic laws and harmonic aesthetic principles. Geoesthesis will be the perceptual mode, *geoesthetics* the guiding principles of a spiritually unified planetary art and science.

Geoesthetics will provide the organizational design of the new planetary social order. Informed by the synchronistic and simultaneous knowing of the noosphere, the new discipline will also provide the means of higher mental or paranormal technologies for cleaning up the environment and transforming waste into art.

The noospherically attuned humans will learn by these new principles to function as terrestrial antennae to moderate the electromagnetic field directly and establish communication with cosmic civilizations throughout the universe. Liberated from the linear concept of time rooted in an arbitrary point in history and returned to living by the great cycles of the universe, the humans will realize time as the principle medium of both art and telepathy. New, undreamed of vistas will be opened for the practice of geoesthetics: Earth will be transformed into a radiant work of art.

16

Passionate Curiosity

The Stance of the Scientist, the Seeker, and the Journalist

ALISON ROSE LEVY

Somewhere, the underlying curiosities, the investigative spirits of the journalist, the scientist, and the seeker all meet.

"I have no special talents. I am only passionately curious," Albert Einstein wrote to a friend, I learned from Arnold Mindell, Ph.D., a Jungian analyst. As a journalist, I can say exactly the same thing. So in this contribution to the debate on science and spirituality, I'll share the questions I am curious about and invite your answers—and your questions.

The reason I do this is because I've noticed an irony. The irony is that when the scientist or the journalist finds answers, the answers must remain open, serving as doorways to further questions that naturally arise in their wake. Without this openness to further questions, these answers, whether scientific findings, reports on slices of reality, or certitudes about how things work, may over time crystallize, become opaque, and begin to function as obstacles, blocking further inquiry into the essence of ever evolving change in the now.

And what about the curiosity of the seeker? Can the long-sought wisdom, once found, also limit? Do our questions about ultimate realities lead us into mystery, only to colonize it with our names or our beliefs? Perhaps religion has inspired so much distrust, conflict, and war because, ultimately, every coat covering infinitude must be shed.

Somehow the hope was that an inward-turning spirituality was innately inhospitable to hardening into the ironclad, established belief system of a religion. After thirty years or more of the current Western "spiritual" movement, we can now take a look and see if that is so. Many spiritual and/or scientific core beliefs are now well articulated and recognized—if not by a majority, at the very least by a very sizeable number of people. Even as we seek to extend that wisdom to others, let's open ourselves to ask whether some of our firmly held tenets, called forth in a past moment, without our noticing, may have grown opaque. Are our favorite tenets of inner spirituality still transparent, or might they have developed into barriers to the changes called forth by this current of time.

For example, does the core of spirituality reside within us in our own inner state? It may be all that most of us can know or experience, but is it all that is?

Is the outer world a mere projection of the sum total of all our states? Or is it a reflection, a barometer, or a feedback loop in which we can see the world we are manifesting and make adjustments in attitude and action? I sometimes sense that the unexplored underbelly of inward-turning spirituality is a hidden belief that the world is on its own trajectory, from which we must retreat to maintain a joyful state. Are we using spiritual understanding as a coping mechanism, as an indispensable safe harbor for remaining sane in a world in disarray or challenge?

Even as we take comfort from spiritual understanding, could that very comfort, that very certitude so shelter us that we evade acting in the moment for its present need, be it restoring the environment, assuring democratic institutions, or safeguarding food, health, and water?

Similar to the instructions given by flight personnel, perhaps it's essential to first don our own "spiritual air mask" before we take action to help others. At what point does that self-care rigidify into something akin to narcissism with a spiritual cast? Is the calling to hear and respond to the cry of the world urgent and reflective of compassion with or without a perfected inner state? Or is it fruitless, ineffective, and driven by the negative emotions of anger and fear until and unless we address those inner tendencies first?

These questions call us to consider another question: Where is the nexus of transformation? For some it seems obvious that the focus is on changing outer reality, other people, or social forces that are having a negative effect on people or on Earth. Whether the focus is on bombing the hell out of a perceived enemy in a distant country or on preserving food, water, and the environment from certain policies or companies, the focus is the same—on an outer world that's a fixer-upper.

Yet many regard these outer concerns as buying into illusion. The outer world is less real than we perceive it to be. As such, the nexus of change resides within. All we can perceive is filtered through our inner state anyway, so it's pointless to seek to act elsewhere.

Within this wide cosmos, it sometimes seems that different people are disposed to seek in different dimensions of this manifestation, inner and outer. Everyone is fascinated by the territory they've mapped out to explore—or been confined to explore.

My question is, Where do the inner and outer meet and cocreate in true integrity and balance? Can we safely omit either inner intention or outer action? And my next question is, Can one genuinely evolve, and is it truly spiritual, to take refuge in the inner domain of the transpersonal without first doing all that is possible to resolve pressing concerns in the outer domain of the personal, the interpersonal, and the collective?

The Nature of Mind and Consciousness

Introduction to Round Five

In his challenging contribution to the science and spirituality discussion Peter Russell again poses the "hard question," How do the workings of the brain's neural networks produce the inner experience we call consciousness? In his answer, he looks at the possibilities opened by neuroscientists regarding the capacity of microtubules and other subneuronal networks. This is also the possibility explored in light of the latest research by psychiatrist and neurophysiologist Ede Frecska. The possibilities opened by such explorations are vast: Russell raises the question of apprehending what the mystics often call the divine, while Frecska suggests the existence of an entire alternative avenue of perception, just as important, or perhaps even more important than the avenue of conventional sensory perception. Amit Goswami in turn speculates that our individual, multiple perceptions of reality may constitute not many, but just one perception: that of unitary consciousness. Consciousness may indeed be just one, and the avenue to discovering it is, for Goswami, through creative evolution.

On a different but pertinent note, Beth Green argues that our attempts to understand what we are and what our consciousness is, whether through science or through spirituality, are in danger of being derailed by the presence of the ego. A clearer, more reliable understanding requires us to free ourselves from the ego-domination of our thoughts and explorations—a task that applies to scientists as well as to spiritual people.

This round raises again some of the most fundamental questions underlying our understanding of the nature of mind and consciousness as well as of ourselves. It thus offers us much food for thought for our own creative evolution as well as for the evolution of our discussions.

17

Consciousness

The Bridge between Science and Spirit

PETER RUSSELL

Science has largely ignored the subject of consciousness, and for seemingly sound reasons. First, consciousness cannot be weighed, measured, or observed in the way that material objects can. Second, scientists have sought to arrive at universal objective truths, truths that are not dependent on an observer's viewpoint or state of mind; they have deliberately avoided subjective considerations. And third, there appears to be no need to explore consciousness; science seems able to explain the functioning of the universe without any need to venture into the perplexing subject of consciousness.

But recent developments in physics, psychology, and neurophysiology are showing that consciousness cannot be quite so easily sidelined, and today a small but growing number of scientists are seeking to account for the existence of consciousness. Some believe that a deeper understanding of brain chemistry will provide the answers. Others look to quantum physics: perhaps the minute microtubules found inside nerve cells create some quantum effects that somehow contribute to consciousness. Some believe that consciousness emerges from the complexity of the processes going on in the brain. Others find sources of hope in chaos theory.

Yet whatever idea is put forward, one thorny question remains: How does any activity or process in the brain result in an inner personal experience? Why doesn't it all go on in the dark, without any awareness? The philosopher David Chalmers has dubbed this the "hard problem" of consciousness. How can something as immaterial as consciousness ever arise from something as unconscious as matter?

The continued failure of these approaches to make any appreciable headway into this problem suggests they all may be on the wrong track. The current scientific worldview holds that the material world—the world of space, time, and matter—is the primary reality. Most scientists therefore assume that awareness emerges from the material world in some way or other. But if this assumption is getting us nowhere, perhaps we should consider the alternative view that awareness—the capacity for inner experience, of whatever kind—is not a product of the material world, but is intrinsic to the cosmos, as fundamental as space, time, and matter.

This suggestion is not new. It is a common theme in Eastern philosophy and is taken seriously by a number of Western philosophers. It also appears in many metaphysical teachings. But Western science has shied away from this idea. It lies too far beyond the current paradigm.

In this alternative view, consciousness does not arise from some particular arrangement of nerve cells or processes going on between them or from any other physical feature; it is always present. All creatures have some form of inner experience. They may not be self-conscious as humans are or have thoughts and emotions, but there is nonetheless some degree of inner awareness, however faint.

Many mystics claim to experience this directly, seeing that the essence of consciousness found within them is the same essence found in all things. Here they find a deep union with all creation.

DISCOVERING THE DIVINE

We can think of mystics as inner scientists—scientists of the mind. Traditional scientists seek to understand a phenomenon through careful observation. They reduce distracting data, or "noise," to a minimum and control factors that may disturb their observations. Then they make deductions from their observations and share their conclusions with others to see if they agree.

Mystics do the same in the realm of mind. They seek to minimize the noise of mental distractions by withdrawing attention from sensory experience, quieting the mind, and focusing on aspects of consciousness that normally pass unnoticed. And they too have shared their findings, not in scientific journals, but in the numerous spiritual teachings and discourses that abound in every culture.

These inner scientists have observed the arising and passing of thought. They have looked to the source of their experience, to the very essence of mind. There they have discovered a profound connection with the ground of all being. The sense of being an individual self— that feeling of "I-ness" that we all know so well but find so hard to define—turns out to be not so unique after all. It is simply the feeling of being aware and is something we share with everyone else. The light of consciousness that I know as me is the same light that you know as you—the same light shining in a myriad of minds.

Some have expressed this inner union in the statement, "I am God." To traditional religion, this rings of blasphemy: How can any lowly human being claim that he or she is God, the almighty supreme being? For modern science, such statements are nothing more than self-delusion. Physicists have looked out into deep space to the edges of the universe, back into "deep time" to the beginning of creation, and down into "deep structure" to the fundamental constituents of matter. In each case they found no evidence for God, nor any need for God. The universe seems to work perfectly well without any divine assistance.

But when mystics speak of the divine, they are not speaking of some supernatural supreme being who rules the workings of the universe;

they are talking of the world within. If we want to find God, we need to look into the realm of "deep mind"—a realm that science has yet to explore.

When science begins to explore the mind as deeply as it has explored matter, it may find it has embarked on a course that will ultimately lead it to discover the divine. To the scientific establishment, rooted in a materialist worldview, this is anathema. But so was the notion of the solar system four centuries ago.

18

The Direct-Intuitive-Nonlocal Mind

Another Foundation for Knowledge?

EDE FRECSKA

Nonlocal information about the physical universe offers the missing link between objective science and subjective experience, including consciousness and spiritual experiences. Based on the principle of nonlocality and with the "quantum array antenna" of subcellular, cytoskeletal networks, the brain can be resonating with the whole universe. The brain may contain the whole cosmos like a quantum hologram, and the perennial wisdom of "As above, so below" (or, "As within, so without"), "The kingdom of Heaven is within you," or "Look within, you are the Buddha," creates the appropriate perspective. The cytoskeletal matrix may be the mediator of the Jungian collective unconscious, and cytoskeletal quantum holography may explain a very common but obscure phenomenon known as intuition.

Ritual ceremonies and other spiritual practices based on the integrative forms of altered states of consciousness (ASCs)—an integrative ASC leads to healing, in contrast with a disintegrative one such as psychosis or drunkenness—elude neuroscientific explanations based on classical cognition. Classical cognition can be conceptualized as a "perceptual-cognitive" way of information processing characteristic of ordinary states of consciousness. This information processing uses the local aspect of the universe and is contrasted with another way of obtaining knowledge, which is based on nonlocal connections, denoted here as a "direct-intuitive" way.

The perceptual-cognitive mode is neuroaxonally based and relies on sensory perception, cognitive processing, and symbolic (visual, verbal, logical-language) mediation. This form of information processing is an indirect mode of achieving knowledge, compared with the direct-intuitive way. In accordance with the indirect nature of its processing, this mode splits the world into subject and object and then performs its modeling. The linguistic feature makes this mode transferable from individual to individual, but at the same time limits it to be culturally bound. The perceptual-cognitive mode of information processing has been evolved for the purpose of task solving, represents a "coping machine" at work, and reaches its peak in Western scientific thinking.

The introduction of a nonlocal, direct-intuitive channel is necessary for an ontological interpretation of integrative ASCs, such as the shamanic or mystic states of consciousness.* We may assume that this mode of accessing knowledge is based on subcellular, cytoskeletal functions, provides direct experience (no subject-object split), and is not bound by language or other symbols. It is practically ineffable, nontransferable. Since the direct-intuitive channel lacks linguistic-symbolic mediation, it has universal characteristics and shows more transcultural similarity, although culture-specific interpretations exist. This may be why mystics get better agreement comparing their "data" than do materialistic scientists. I am not arguing here for the ontological validation of every experience in ASCs, but for a few, very informative experiences that constitute the integrative ASCs.

The direct-intuitive perception of the world carries a high degree of

---

*See Rick Strassman, Slawek Wojtowicz-Praga, Luis E. Luna, and Ede Frecska. *Inner Paths to Outer Space* (Rochester, Vt.: Inner Traditions, 2007).

uncertainty and needs rigorous training for its highest development—as in other fields. It takes decades to train an indigenous shaman or Buddhist monk because the direct-intuitive route into the realm of non-ordinary consciousness is seemingly capricious, its denizens are unpredictable, and our perceptual-cognitive mind is unprepared to face its challenges. What can be nourished can be atrophied as well; the latter happened in Western civilization, and the direct-intuitive channel has become "the forgotten knowledge." It might have been the source of ancient myths. Giving credit to mythical knowledge also means that the teachings of ancient myths and wisdom traditions should be considered starting points for the development of modern scientific theories and deserve to be treated as working hypotheses in applying the scientific method.

The perceptual-cognitive foundation of knowledge is a result of the brain's interactions with the local aspects of the universe. The direct-intuitive perception of the world derives from the nonlocal features of the cosmos. In other words, the local universe of the classical, Newtonian worldview is the reality of our ordinary consciousness, based on the perceptual-cognitive process. On the other hand, the brain's interfacing with the nonlocal universe generates the reality of nonordinary states. Moreover, as will be outlined below, the direct-intuitive way is also the source of the subjective component of our consciousness. My main point is that intuition, consciousness, and nonlocality are interwoven.

"*COGITO*" UPDATED

The basic principles of the second foundation of knowledge (the direct-intuitive-nonlocal) can shed light on peculiar features of consciousness and on what various cultural views and wisdom traditions attribute to it. For example, the indigenous Arawate people of the Amazon state that from the jaguars' perspective, they are the people and we are the jaguars. In essence, jaguars are conscious beings. Aside from questions of ignorance, how can rational thinking make sense of such a statement? How is it that there are traditions that connect consciousness with beings and inanimate objects other than the human brain? The following passage may help to interpret these concepts and the principles of *panpsychic* and *hylozoic* views.

As a starting point I refer to Ervin Laszlo, who had the notion what I wish to build on: "What we call 'matter' is the aspect we apprehend when we look at a person, a plant, or a molecule from the outside; 'mind' is the aspect we obtain when we look at the same thing from the inside."* For me it means that if we use the perceptual-cognitive approach—the "outsider" approach—then everything is seen as an object without consciousness. How do we relate to our brain from inside; how do we perceive our own consciousness? Naturally, we cannot see, touch, or smell our own or others' minds. We are left only with the other approach, the nonlocal, direct-intuitive mode of knowing that is the method of looking at things from the inside. The intuitive apprehension is the way for us to recognize that we are conscious. All of us have a direct, intuitive knowledge of our own consciousness and not a perceptual one.

At the base of the yet-dominant Newtonian-Cartesian worldview stands Descartes's *Cogito, ergo sum* ("I think, therefore I am"). It presupposes another question: How do I know about myself? Turning Descartes' coin to the other side, we can say, "I am aware of myself, therefore (or because) I am intuitive." That means I have a way of getting knowledge without the senses, without using local processes of nature. This leaves me with the other, the nonlocal mode of apprehension.

My conclusion may sound trivial, yet it carries nontrivial consequences. The direct-intuitive approach is a way we relate to things from their inside. In the eye of the "insider"—as Ervin Laszlo pointed out eloquently—we always sense the presence of consciousness.

---

*See Ervin Laszlo, *Science and the Akashic Field: An Integral Theory of Everything* (Rochester, Vt.: Inner Traditions, 2007).

Consequently, intuition, nonlocality, and consciousness seem to be intimately related. We can have intuitive knowledge without awareness of its source. However, if we are aware of its origin then we can attribute consciousness to the source *in nascendi*. In this regard Stuart Hameroff is right: subneural structures (which serve as the interface for the direct-intuitive mode of information processing) mediate consciousness.* I would add that these structures mediate not only our consciousness, but also the consciousness of every entity to which we relate intuitively.

What follows next is a generalization: the same way I attribute consciousness to myself, I can attribute it to everything else via the direct-intuitive approach since consciousness arises during the intuitive process. Our perceptual reality consists of material objects, while the world of intuition is filled with conscious entities. Animals, plants, even rocks or the whole universe are conscious. They can be felt to be that in an integrative ASC, which has the nonlocal, direct-intuitive approach as its *modus operandi*. The eternal philosophical debate over the priority of consciousness or matter seems to me to be transcended by the recognition of the reality of nonlocal and local processes. Consciousness and matter are attributes that depend only on the way we obtain our knowledge.

---

*See Stuart Hameroff, *Ultimate Computing* (Amsterdam: North-Holland, 1987).

19

The Real Secret of How We Create Our Own Reality

AMIT GOSWAMI

Certain spiritual teachings can be very confusing when we first hear them, whether we are scientists or not. When back in the 1970s, the physicist Fred Alan Wolf created the evocative phrase, "We create our own reality," it sounded good, but gave rise to many disappointments. People tried to manifest fancy automobiles, vegetable gardens in desert environments, or parking spaces in busy downtown areas. Wolf based his phrase on the work of mathematician John von Neumann, who first introduced the idea of the "collapse" of consciousness, which occurs when the quantum wave of possibility "chooses" one of its facets, which then becomes actualized.

Yet many attempts to follow through and create our own reality produced a mixed bag of outcomes because the would-be creators were unaware of something important: we create our own reality, yes, but we don't do that in our ordinary state of consciousness, but in a *nonordinary* state of consciousness. The paradox of Wigner's friend, articulated by Eugene Wigner, a Nobel laureate physicist, helps to clarify this.

Wigner approaches a quantum traffic light that offers two possibilities: red and green. Simultaneously, Wigner's friend approaches the same light from the road perpendicular to Wigner's. They both choose green, but their choices are contradictory. If both choices materialize at the same time, there would be pandemonium. Obviously, only one of them gets to choose, but who?

An understanding of narcissism offers an insight as we go about trying to create our own reality. How could it be that only one person in the world is sentient and the rest of us only exist within this person's imagination?

Three physicists independently resolved Wigner's paradox. They were Ludwig Bass in Australia, myself at Oregon, and Casey Blood at Rutgers in New Jersey. The solution was simply this: consciousness is one, nonlocal, and cosmic, behind the local individuality of Wigner and his friend. Although both men want the green light, the one consciousness chooses for both of them, avoiding any contradiction. The one consciousness chooses such that the result dictated by quantum probability calculations is validated: Wigner and his friend each get green 50 percent of the time. Yet for any individual crossing, a creative opportunity for getting green is left open for each.

In formulating my theory about this, the underlying question was, What is the nature of consciousness that enables it to be the free agent of downward causation without any paradox?

The answer was that consciousness has to be unitive, one and only for all of us. This oneness of consciousness is the basis of our theories about it.

When my paper proclaiming this was published back in 1989, University of Mexico neurophysiologist Jacobo Grinberg-Zylberbaum noticed it. Grinberg-Zylberbaum was studying novel transfers of electrical brain activity between two people. Intuiting that my theory was relevant to his research, he asked me to visit his laboratory, check out his experimental setup, and check the data to help him interpret them. Soon Grinberg-Zylberbaum and his collaborators wrote the first paper proclaiming a modern scientific verification of the idea of oneness of consciousness.

THE GOOD NEWS EXPERIMENT:
WE *ARE* ONE?

Since then, four separate experiments have shown that quantum consciousness, the author of downward causation, is nonlocal and unitive. Quantum physics provides an amazing principle to operate with—nonlocality. The principle of locality says that all communication must proceed through local signals with speed limits. Albert Einstein established the speed of light as the speed limit. This precludes instantaneous communication via signals. Yet, quantum objects *are* able to influence one another instantly once they interact and become correlated through quantum nonlocality. In 1982, physicist Alain Aspect and his collaborators confirmed this with a pair of photons (quanta of light). There's no contradiction to Einsteinian thinking once we recognize quantum nonlocality for what it is—a signal-less interconnectedness outside space and time.

Grinberg-Zylberbaum, in 1993, was trying to demonstrate quantum nonlocality for two correlated brains. In his experiment, two people meditate together with the intention of direct (signal-less, nonlocal) communication. After twenty minutes, they are separated (while still continuing their unifying intention), placed in individual Faraday cages (electromagnetically impervious chambers), and each brain is wired up to an electroencephalogram (EEG) machine. One subject is shown a series of light flashes, producing in his or her brain an electrical activity that is recorded in the EEG machine, and this brain activity produces an "evoked potential," which is extracted by a computer from the brain noise. Surprisingly, the same evoked potential is found to appear in the other subject's brain and is viewable on the EEG of this subject (again minus brain noise). This is called a "transferred potential" but is similar to the evoked potential in phase and strength. Control subjects (those who neither meditate together nor hold the intention for signal-less communication during the duration of the experiment) do not show any transferred potential.

Obviously, the experiment demonstrates the nonlocality of brain responses, but it also demonstrates the nonlocality of quantum consciousness. How else to explain how the *forced* choice of the evoked response in one subject's brain can lead to the *free* choice of an (almost) identical response in the correlated partner's brain? The experiment has been replicated several times since then, by neuropsychiatrist Peter Fenwick and collaborators in 1998 in London, by Jiri Wackermann and colleagues in 2003, and by Bastyr University researcher Leana Standish and her collaborators in 2004.

The conclusion derived from these experiments is radical and can integrate science and spirituality, Vedanta-style. Quantum consciousness, the precipitator of the downward causation of choice from quantum possibilities, is what esoteric spiritual traditions within many cultures call God (in Sanskrit, Ishwara.) In a sense, we have rediscovered God within science. However it is within a new paradigm of science, based not on the primacy of matter as in the old science, but on the primacy of consciousness. Consciousness is the ground of all being that we now can recognize as what the spiritual tradition of Vedanta calls Brahma and what esoteric Christianity calls Godhead, or Christ.

THE POWER OF INTENTION

Grinberg-Zylberbaum's experiment also demonstrates the power of our intention, which parapsychologist Dean Radin has also studied. One of Radin's experiments took place during the O. J. Simpson trial, when many people were watching the trial on TV. Radin correctly hypothesized that the intentions of the viewing audience would widely fluctuate depending on whether the courtroom drama was intense or ho-hum. This activity, he theorized, might influence random number generators. Radin asked a group of psychologists to plot and note down in real time the intensity of the courtroom drama. Meanwhile, in the laboratory, Radin measured the deviations of random number generators. He found that the random number generators maximally deviated from randomness precisely when the courtroom drama was high. What does this mean? The philosopher Gregory Bateson said, "The opposite of randomness is choice." So the correlation proves the creative power of intention.

In another series of experiments, Radin found that random number generators deviate from randomness in meditation halls when people meditate together (showing high intention), but not at a corporate board meeting!

I'll bet you're wondering how to develop the power of intention. We all try to manifest things through our intentions; sometimes they work, but less often than not. This is because we are in our ego, rather than higher consciousness, when we intend. But how do we change that?

I propose a four-stage process: An intention must start with the ego since that is where we ordinarily are—local, selfish. At the second stage, we intend for everyone to go beyond selfishness. We don't need to worry, since we haven't lost anything. When we say "everyone," that includes *us,* too. In the third stage, we allow our intentions to become a prayer: if my intention resonates with the intention of the whole, of quantum consciousness, then let it come to fruition. At the fourth stage, the prayer must pass into silence, must become a meditation.

You may have seen a recent movie, *The Secret,* or have read a book by the same name. They talk about the secret of manifestation through our intention. The main message is good. To manifest, the book and the movie teach us, not only do we have to actively intend, but we also have to learn to passively wait. Maybe the intended object will come to us. That's why I too recommend that we end in silence, waiting.

If we wait too long, however, we may forget what we were intending. So we cut short the waiting and become active again in our search. In this way the real secret of manifestation is an alternation between doing and being. I sometimes call this a "do-be-do-be-do" lifestyle. In India, people are in a "be-be-be" lifestyle, haven't you noticed? In America and the West, of course, it is "do-do-do." The connoisseur of manifestation via intention making takes the middle path, "do-be-do-be-do."

There is one final secret question: How do we know what consciousness intends so we can align our intention with it? The answer is creative evolution. Consciousness intends to evolve us toward greater good for everyone through creative evolution.

20

Reclaiming Science and Spirituality from the Ego

BETH GREEN

A young child stares at the stars with wonder. That child might become a scientist, a mystic, or both. A young person feels the suffering of others and wonders what can be done. That child might become a doctor or a healer. Wonder motivates inquiry, and the desire to help turns our intentions toward the alleviation of suffering and to the pursuit of progress, either through scientific or spiritual means.

Whichever metaphor we choose to explore, science or spirituality, whichever path we choose to alleviate suffering, the material or spiritual, whether as a physicist or mystic, an environmentalist or intuitive counselor, we face the same questions: How does self-interest derail both the wonder and the desire to help? How have our initial impulses been hijacked by the ego, and what can we do about it?

Ego is the awareness of individual existence. It is natural and part of the human condition, yet in its immature form, it compels us toward behaviors that are self-serving and shortsighted. The child who loves chemistry is praised by the science teacher, who is equally validated by that child's interest. Ego is already at work. Now the child begins competing to be the best, to achieve, and to gain recognition. Later, he or she competes for scholarships, professorships, placement in scientific journals, grants, prizes, recognition. How many of us can stand up to that kind of environment and not be influenced in the choices we make, choices as to what to study, how to present ourselves, who to credit, and who not to credit? How many of us can stand up to the ego's endless craving for recognition, praise, and validation? Pride in ourselves begins to trump wonder.

Scientists jockeying for power and position are unconsciously propelled in directions that may not benefit science or the planet Earth. At conferences, "me-based" agendas begin to seep into our conversations as we choose the paths that either feed our pride or our pocketbooks. Some of us, whose egos are fed more by defiance, will find controversial ways to stand out. Those whose egos are fed by acceptance seek peer recognition. We have many rationalizations. I have a family to feed. I need to establish my credibility in my field. I need to build my department, my institute. Who is completely disengaged from these considerations? How many of us are totally focused on the end goals? What will support the whole? How can I make the greatest contribution?

In the spiritual sphere, it is no different. An intuitive counselor lives every day in the reality of oneness. Where do we get our information as intuitives, except through our connection either to the psyche of another or to higher consciousness itself? Yet we who live every day in the reality of oneness will jockey for recognition among our peers. Where is oneness now?

As a spiritual teacher, if I teach a message that makes me popular, won't I ignore the imperative of a different message, one that will turn people away, all the time rationalizing that I am teaching the truth or this is what people need now? If I am rewarded for puffing up the egos of my followers, won't I unconsciously gravitate toward making people feel good? If I am rewarded for tearing people down, won't I ultimately become a caricature of toughness and of myself?

The ego creates agendas not only for our personal self-aggrandizement, but also for our personal and collective domination of other beings, other species, and life itself. It is well-known that science has been used to manipulate, dominate, and create profit through the application of science to weaponry and to the creation of vehicles that damage the environment. And spirituality is being used in the same ways, even in its new age form. Whether we use voodoo to damage our enemies, prayers to win games, or spiritual laws to attract prosperity, our egos determine what should happen, and we attempt to apply spiritual power to meet those agendas. Instead of spirituality being an outreach to the universe, it becomes a way of dominating it. And, of course, the masses of folks, who are also dominated by ego, will applaud.

There is nothing wrong with asking science or spirituality to improve our lives, but only from a place of wonder and service to the whole, and that is anathema to the ego, which is focused on me-based, short-term goals. How do we free ourselves from the domination of the ego so that once more science and spirituality are a sacred trust, committed to wonder, inquiry, and cocreation with the universe of which we are a part?

We acknowledge the devastating impact of the ego on our souls, our society, and our environment.

We examine our beliefs and behaviors and ask ourselves whether we are acting for the highest good of all, including ourselves, or focusing on agendas for validation, admiration, attention, power, or success.

Once we have acknowledged how much we are run by ego, we laugh.

We recollect the wonder and/or the devotion to service that once inspired us and reconnect to that passion.

We retrain ourselves to think in terms of the whole, remembering that we can only thrive when everyone and everything is thriving.

We remember God.

Recently Stephen Hawking asserted that science does not need God to explain existence. That may be true, but we need God, the source, the higher consciousness, to stop ourselves from destroying it. Without God, our egos become God, and we have seen the results.

Once we looked up at the stars and felt uplifted by belonging to the infinite. That is the deepest joy of any human being, to be part of something greater than ourselves. But that something that is greater than ourselves cannot be limited to our family, community, religion, nation, race, or even species. We belong to God, to the universe of which we are a part. And when we feel the power of that belonging, the ego cannot dominate, and it must evolve.

Crisis
and
Spirituality

Introduction to Round Six

Not surprisingly, Round Six of our conversation is dedicated to exploring the relationship between science and spirituality and the possibilities of bridging the gap that separates them. The focus is also on the crisis in the world that calls for a little-used resource to face and overcome it: spirituality.

Institute of Noetic Sciences President and CEO Marilyn Mandala Schlitz frames the question of making use of the power of spirituality to open the path to a better future in terms of the images we have of ourselves and humankind. The "dominator" image of the recent past has lost its focus. Sudden cataclysmic events like the Japanese quake and tsunami, coupled with social and political unrest in the Middle East, have shaken our belief in certainty. We realize that we are close to a tipping point and that now we also need to realize that it is up to us to decide which way the world will tip. We need to develop a higher grade of resilience in the face of crises and adversity. History tells us that we are a resilient species, possessing creative insight and the potential for life-enhancing breakthroughs. We need an expanded vision to give us greater resilience to face the challenges that await all of us in the very near future.

James O'Dea, the next eloquent voice in our round, assures us that spirituality is a moral force. We live in a fundamentally moral universe. Morality is the template of human consciousness. A healthy individual with a sound consciousness is a moral individual, recognizing his or her true nature as a being in a moral universe. What we need is not more skill and cleverness in devising desperate measures to correct problems created by a faulty consciousness, but to recognize that life itself arises from order, beauty, and truth in nature. A return to nature is a return to the morality inherent in the cosmos. It is the way forward in our crisis-ridden world.

Another underused and nearly unrecognized resource is the power of the words we pronounce. Japanese spiritual leader Masami Saionji tells us that pure energy always emanates from the source of the universe, and we can all access it. How we use it determines our future, and even the future of our world. Positive utterances create a positive field around us, and this also affects other people's decisions, behaviors, relationships, and even their bodily and mental health. Negative utterances do the exact opposite: they create negative fields that can even kill. In the final count it is our level of consciousness that determines how we act and, by that token, which future awaits us. The highest form of consciousness is "universal consciousness," where we are one with nature and all life. Achieving this level of consciousness restores our original power to heal ourselves and heal the world.

Indian educator Jagdish Gandhi agrees with this in the final piece for this round. If we wish to live in a better society, we must achieve a higher level of consciousness—a consciousness tempered with morality—and the promotion of this level of consciousness calls for educating our children. If we bring about a compassionate, just, and dedicated generation of children, we do our duty. There are many examples of such a consciousness emerging today among children who do not wait for their elders to take the initiative but are themselves ready to push for change. Our fate is in the hands of our children, yet it is ultimately in our hands, for it is up to us to help children to develop the consciousness that can empower them to change the world.

The paramount insight emerging in these insightful papers

regarding spirituality and the human future is that spirituality is a key resource in our endeavor to shape the future. It is not something outside or beyond nature, not something artificial that we dream up and fabricate. It is there as a fundamental principle in the universe. We only need to recognize it to enhance our consciousness, and with a higher consciousness we can act in a way that can rebalance our off-balance civilization—for our sake and for the sake of our children and their children.

21

A Path Forward

Embracing Our Creative Imagination

MARILYN MANDALA SCHLITZ

It's been quite a year—and it's only March (2011). Extreme political unrest is underway throughout the Middle East. Earthquakes rock New Zealand, China, California, and Japan. Shifting plates and tsunami waves in the Pacific Ocean have nuclear power plants perched on the edge of explosion.

Like many, I track these global events through social media. I'm overwhelmed by the graphic images that are communicated through video links and real-time postings. The Twitter feeds about the earthquake in Japan move so rapidly I can't follow more than fragments of what is being shared. Fearful talk of the next Armageddon is couched in the language of 2012 and divine retribution. I feel breathless at the pace of horror and destruction. I'm reminded of that old joke about the conflict between the pessimist and the optimist. The pessimist says, "It can't get worse." The optimist responds, "Oh yes it can."

Looking to both science and spirituality, how can we find what Stanford psychologist Phillip Zimbardo calls the "heroic imagination"? What do we need to avoid the slippery slope of despair? Avoiding groupthink and the negativity of the media can be tricky as we seek the hero within us to overcome fear and affect positive change.

Our cultural stories—and the images we hold about possible futures—shape the path we take forward. As noted in a report called "Changing Images of Man," written several decades ago by former Institute of Noetic Sciences President Willis Harman and his colleagues at SRI International, "Images of humankind that are dominant in a culture are of fundamental importance because they underlie the ways in which the society shapes its institutions, educates its young, and goes about whatever it perceives its business to be. Changes in these images are of particular concern at the present time because our industrial society may be on the threshold of a transformation as profound as that which came to Europe when the Medieval Age gave way to the rise of science and the Industrial Revolution."

Such sage insight speaks to the dominant image that drives economic growth and our efforts to control the forces of an objective world "out" there. Now, well into a new era of information, globalization, and quantum interconnections, the "dominator" image has lost its focus. Events like the recent tsunami shake our certainty. We are being forced to examine our deepest assumptions about what is real and true.

In this process, new images are emerging to guide us. Research shows that crisis is a great catalyst for positive transformations. Even when things are painful, we have the capacity to make shifts in our worldview and recalibrate our belief systems. We may begin to see ourselves as part of a living system—moving with the flow of evolution rather than thinking we can dominate over it.

Futurists today tell us we are at a kind of tipping point. It's just not clear which way things are tipping. On the one hand, we may be on the verge of a full-systems collapse. On the other, we may be heading for the rebirth of a sustainable society. To find our way to this second option, we are well served to follow the advice of former writer and aikido master George Leonard to "take the hit as a gift."

Futurist Oliver Markley has long been calling for a new image for our shared humanity. In a recent essay in the online journal *Noetic Now* called "Staying Resilient in a Wild-Card World," he argues that we need to keep a 360-degree perspective when anticipating trends and types of change. Most futures research focuses on relatively probable future patterns. These relate to outcomes that are either feared or desired. But another important catalyst for change is what are called wild-card events. These include low-probability events (Wild Card I) that are unlikely to occur (a massive earthquake and tsunami ravaging Japan) and high-probability events that don't fit into current thinking (Wild Card II) and so carry low credibility (as was the case with climate change and now could be argued for the unanticipated crisis of Japan's nuclear plants). Both can lead to unanticipated consequences that result in highly disruptive impacts.

A soft-spoken but big-vision futurist, Markley argues for the importance of guiding images to shape these possible futures. In his words, "Such shifts are increasingly being seen by experts as unlikely to emerge unless profound crises first occur that disintegrate the orderly functioning of existing societal systems. At the same time, it is hypothesized that the avoidance of profound civilizational collapse and evolution toward more benign alternative future possibilities, where resiliently sustainable socioecological systems can flourish, will be strongly shaped by the extent to which appropriate *new* guiding images quickly become an essential part of the zeitgeist."

Markley identifies *resilience* as a key transition-informing principle. Grounded in complexity theory, the focus on resilience addresses natural cycles of growth and dissolution. Markley draws on the Resilience Project, an interdisciplinary effort that uses diverse approaches to the study of how families, children, and youth can develop resilience in the face of adversity. The focus of this program is the study of the social and physical ecologies that make resilience more likely to occur.

Resilience research is grounded in what futurists call *panarchy theory*. At the core of this theory is an *adaptive cycle,* which shapes the responses of individuals, institutions, and ecosystems to crises. Reaching a stage of vulnerability can lead to historically significant global transformation. But will this transformation be one that supports the future of life on our planet?

As noted in Markley's article, Duncan and Graeme Taylor are futurists who have considered this question. In their article, "The Collapse and Transformation of Our World,"* they argue that we may be facing two possible futures. One involves an inclusive (sustainable) solution that can lead to a constructive reorganization of society. The other is a solution that will lead to conflicts over scarce resources and the disintegration of global civilization.

Which future manifests is based on how credible people find the cause to take action and on their trust of their own self-efficacy. The threat of disaster, without an image of better possible outcomes, can lead people to shut down and deny the problem or its positive resolution. The barriers to positive transformation are real and problematic. But history is a good indicator that we are a resilient species, filled with creative insight and the potential for life-enhancing breakthroughs.

In the face of our current global crises, an expanded sense of perspective, grounded in pragmatic hope, is what is called for. We need to create images that mark a new beginning, expressed in shared intention and collective action. We can do this by finding the hero within each of us. By harnessing our inner capacities, through meditation, contemplation, prayer, and time in nature, we can cultivate the resilience to navigate the challenges of our outer world. Out of catastrophe can come the renewal of civilization. Moving away from reactivity, fear, and panic and toward emotional balance and positive collective actions allows us to apply the time-tested tools for sustaining our well-being. In this process, we can promote deep healing—both individually and for our shared humanity.

---

*See Duncan M. Taylor and Graeme M. Taylor, *Journal of Future Studies* 11, no. 3 (2007): 29–46.

22

Entropy, Negentropy, and Our Moral Imagination

JAMES O'DEA

Scientists are not the only ones these days pointing out the fact that our planetary civilization is hugely entropic: we are burning up useable stuff at ever accelerating rates. China's latest move to reduce the exporting of rare minerals used for all our tech toys from iPads to cell phones is just our most recent reminder that a lot of Earth's resources that we are pumping, mining, chopping, consuming, burning, eroding, and evaporating will not be available to us in the future. The world economy is built on this irreversible loss of useable energy, and the latest global forecasts indicate that a number of developing countries are really cranking up to get in on the profits to be made in the entropy game. Even if we didn't have residual toxins, pollution, and climate impact, we would still be heading toward the scarcity of useable resources. Some, the Pentagon among them, predict that the next big conflicts will not be over ideology, religion, or land per se but over water, gas, minerals, and, potentially, food.

We have told ourselves that the road out of ruinous poverty and toward sustainable nationhood with the capital resources to fund health care, education, housing, and employment is more trade and more consumption—sell more stuff, use more stuff, burn more stuff, and you will be on your way to thriving.

There are theorists who argue that the only way to stop this deficit consumption of Earth's useable energy is to redesign the entire global economic order so that it moves from entropy to entropic balance. Systems that balance their energy loss with the intake of fresh energy maintain equilibrium. Nature is our teacher here because it does a brilliant job at using life and the products of life to create more life and sustain life to an incredible degree of abundance. Until we came along and raided the abundance and created huge entropy deficits!

I cannot tell you whether we can employ greening strategies at the kind of speed necessary to make proper use of natural flowlike wave, wind, and solar radiation at a scale needed for 7 to 8 billion people. Or that we can rapidly ramp up recycling initiatives that not only recycle our trash but also rebuild our homes, offices, furniture, clothes, vehicles, and so on. If it is possible to reach negentropic equilibrium using fast-track greening strategies, it would require a fundamental moral choice to redesign the present so that we do not place our unsustainable deficit energy consumption on the backs of future generations and seriously compromise their capacity to survive. But this is where I go out on a limb.

If, in fact, the moral construct is as simple and as cogent as "unto the seventh generation," as conveyed in Native American traditions, then we would have a liberating directive to end the injunction to make myopic choices based on the need for immediate profit. I contend that we live in a moral universe and that moral principles are axial templates within consciousness itself: they are the master templates of wisdom, they are the codes for nature's abundance, they are the latent possibilities for endless ingenuity and creativity, and they are design fractals that guide the evolution of higher consciousness in human beings.

At root, what is needed is our moral development as a species and not more dazzling displays of cleverness funded by greed or desperate measures to correct the negative impact of ongoing behavior that is essentially devoid of conscience. Moral development is not about petty strictures but about our greatest asset, which is harnessing the power of imagination in service to ideals worthy of those who truly care about the future. Life itself emerges from principles of order, beauty, and truth, and when we attempt to hijack those principles we create disorder and invert truth and beauty.

Consciousness is still our most spectacular resource, which will open up more energy for our use than we ever imagined possible. But it is not for sale; its highest resources, which may be limitless, are only available to those dedicated to serve, not steal from, the evolving story of life.

Consciousness is not a neutral playground where we create our own realities. It could never be coherent if that were the case, and it would devolve into a universe of competing realities. Dictatorship is precisely the form of subjective manifestation that divorces itself from moral principles, with dire consequences. We do not hand over control of the household to a two-year-old and acclaim the power of the infant to create a reality! But when one returns to the notion that it is inherently a moral universe, then there are consequences to subjectively induced states of mind and forms of action. The moral core of the universe produced the exquisite balance for life on Earth, with its harmony and unfathomable beauty. Only a moral imagination can restore what our immoral greed and flagrant excess have wrecked.

Francis Bacon is the one who said that we must "put Nature on the rack" and torture her until she reveal her secrets. Well, we have done that, and the reality we have created has resemblances to hell. But the reverse is also true: honor and serve the holy order of nature, and vow to serve the cause of life, and she will let us know that our entropy issues are but a speck of dust in the ocean of her creativity.

23

Guiding Our Inner Evolution

MASAMI SAIONJI

Why is it that humanity has not yet made the transition from a materialistic society to one based on principles of harmony, respect, and love? I believe it is because most human beings have been living in ignorance of the truth. We may have acquired much knowledge and information, but the majority of people on Earth do not have a clear understanding about their own existence. Thus, although the solutions to the world's problems are actually in our hands, we cannot see them because we are blinded by our fixed self-perception.

Every human being possesses a creative capacity. Pure energy is always emanating from the source of the universe, and each of us receives a steady supply of this energy. How we use it from moment to moment determines our own future and the future of the world. This universal energy has infinite potential. Each of us assigns a shape to that energy by means of our thoughts and words. This is the process of creation.

The thoughts, words, and emotions that human beings emit each moment are constantly streaming forth from their bodies as creative energy. Each thought, word, and emotion holds its own unique vibration. And those having a similar frequency band together to form a creative field. When the energy of a particular creative field has accumulated to a critical point, it manifests itself on the visible plane in one way or the other.

From what I observe, there are many different kinds of creative fields. For example, there are creative fields with positive energy, such as fields for compassion, optimism, dignity, sincerity, courage, gratitude, peace, and forgiveness. On the other hand, there are creative fields with negative energy, such as fields for anger, fear, pessimism, anxiety, self-hate, suicide, discrimination, and revenge.

As a creative field continues to grow in size, it exerts a stronger and stronger influence on people emitting similar thoughts. It will affect people's decisions, behavior, relationships, and health conditions. And on a larger scale, it could even manifest in the form of war or natural disaster.

Words, in particular, are a concentrated form of energy and a powerful means of creation. Much has been written and said about the creative power of words. But it seems to me that few people truly understand this power. Words are actually alive. Words attract people. Words motivate people. Words are infectious. And words also have sharp edges. Words can give life. And words can even kill.

We must take responsibility for every word we utter. Our first step is to steadily monitor the words we spew out carelessly out of habit. Next, we should train ourselves to intentionally replace the negative words with positive ones. With firm determination, we should resolve to create an entirely new habit by rerecording only positive words over the old tape playing in our conscious and subconscious mind. By doing so, we can change the outcome of our own future and, at the same time, pour positive energy into humanity's collective consciousness.

The point I want to emphasize is this: everything that happens and manifests in this world is of our own making. It is the responsibility of each and every member of humanity. The pattern seen in an individual is reflected in that person's family, which in turn is reflected in his community, in his country, and ultimately in the world. Everything starts from the individual.

The individuals' level of consciousness determines the level of consciousness of humanity as a whole. If one person achieves higher consciousness, the collective consciousness of humanity is uplifted by that much.

As I see it, the choices that people make fall into three broad categories according to their level of consciousness. These three levels are the materialistic consciousness, the spiritual consciousness, and what I call the "universal consciousness."

When we are at the level of materialistic consciousness, we make choices based on ego and greed for the best interests of ourselves, our own families, and our countries.

Then, when we are at the next level, namely the spiritual consciousness, we choose to share with others. We respect and love others and treat them as we would treat ourselves.

An even higher level is the universal consciousness. When we have entered this level, there is no longer any separation between the self and others. We are in oneness with nature and all of life. We will have restored our original power to heal ourselves and our planet.

Up till now, humanity has been driven by materialistic consciousness for the most part. In fear of scarcity, we have continued to pursue material gain from the outer world, taking from others and depleting Earth's natural resources. If we continue on this path, our world will no doubt be headed for destruction.

So, which way should we go forward? If we are to make the right decisions and change the course of humanity, each of us must evolve our consciousness, from materialistic to spiritual and eventually to universal consciousness. Yes, humanity is entering the age of conscious evolution, and we must guide it consciously and purposefully.

In order to do so, we must ask ourselves the ultimate questions: "Who am I," and, "What is the meaning of my existence on Earth?" Each and every one of us must face up to these inevitable questions and find a clear answer to them. To know one's true self is the key to understanding the mysteries of the cosmos. In other words, if we delve deep into the nature of consciousness, we would begin to see the whole picture of the vast universe.

The true essence of our life is connected to the source of the universe. When we rediscover that connection and align our intentions with the harmonious universal intention, we will be supported by a marvelous influx of a higher-dimensional universal energy, which cannot be accessed otherwise.

So let us believe in our potential for building a peaceful and sustainable future for all life on Earth. As more and more people contribute to the creative field of our positive vision with their intentions and positive words, it will surely grow larger and more powerful. Together, we can overturn the old destructive patterns, and humanity shall evolve to new heights.

May peace prevail on Earth.

24

Changing Direction

JAGDISH GANDHI

The world is going through a crisis. Although most governments have pledged themselves to help develop a peaceful, sustainable, and socially just world, still we seem to be going in the opposite direction. Climate scientists have been warning that we are about to cross the tipping point, yet deforestation and environmental degradation continue unchecked. It is almost as if humankind has been gripped by a collective death wish. Though this is a time of great danger, fortunately it is also a time of great opportunity. Today, we have the knowledge and resources to create a peaceful and vibrant world.

A sustainable global system is not an option; it is the requirement if we are to survive as a species. We need to change our global system because the present system itself is the problem. A system designed to promote endless growth through mindless consumption is like a cancer that will ultimately consume humanity. If the present trends continue, growing shortages of water, food, and energy will collapse the global economy. We need a systemic transformation because a consumer society cannot evolve into a conserver society without structural change.

It is no longer a cliché to say that humanity stands at a crossroads. We have two paths to the future. If we continue on the present path we shall destroy our civilization within decades, but if we can visualize the alternative, sustainable model of development, we shall bring about perhaps the most golden of all ages in human history. For this we need to give up the present model of profits at any cost and replace it with one where a holistic approach seeks to create a win-win, sustainable solution to problems by eliminating the underlying causes.

The industrial age has been a necessary stage in human development, enabling us to develop our science and technology. It has resulted in a better and longer life for most people, but these benefits have come at enormous societal and environmental costs. We need to replace the present global system where nation states compete with each other with a new, cooperating planetary civilization.

So how do we go about setting right the wrongs? A greater consciousness is needed. A consciousness that makes us realize that we are only trustees for future generations. A consciousness that tells us that though we can enjoy the bounties of nature, we cannot act in greed. And when this consciousness is tempered with morality, that is, ideal behavior, we will have a better future to look forward to.

If we can all agree that all humans wish to live in an ideal society, then all humans must have a higher consciousness. In societies where this consciousness (a concern for our world and its inhabitants) is ingrained in the mind of an individual right from childhood, it is not difficult to find people who are genuinely concerned about the state of their world. When we see the pitiful condition in which the world finds itself today, we are even more convinced that it is only through education that society can be enriched and given direction. Therefore, education must also act as a powerful instrument for profound social transformation.

Educating society for educating the world starts with educating our children. If we could create a God-loving, compassionate, just, self-sacrificing generation of children, we would have done our duty. The challenge is to change mind-sets so that people in the schools, at home, and in society can collaborate and find solutions to the problems humanity faces today. The paradox is that a child learns something in school and then something completely different when he returns home. In addition, society confuses him even more. It is only when a child learns to differentiate between right and wrong that we can call him a conscious and moral human being. The world needs a generation of such children. Only those children, who grow up and successfully take their rightful place as leaders of society, can bring real peace to the world through their actions.

History is replete with examples of how conscious and morally upright men and women have changed the lives of their fellow beings. Abraham Lincoln, Swami Vivekananda, Mahatma Gandhi, Martin Luther King Jr., Nelson Mandela, and countless others provided inspiration and hopes for generations of change-makers. Perhaps the world is today short of leaders who think and work for the common good of all nations and peoples of the world. What can the children of this world expect from their elders? I suppose it would be best to leave this question unanswered.

Fortunately, we have many inspiring examples of young children who are not willing to wait for the elders to take the initiative but are themselves pushing for change. Like thirteen-year-old Felix Finkbeiner, who, as a nine year old, pledged to plant one million trees. At the age of twelve, he fulfilled his dream by inspiring children in seventy countries, who together planted more than one million trees. Invited to speak to the United Nations General Assembly on February 2 of this year (2011), he said that children no longer trusted the adults who threaten the children's future.

We urgently need to change direction. We must transform our consumer society into a regenerative society where the focus is not on having more but on being more. There is no third option; societies and species that are not environmentally sustainable become extinct. Our fate is in our hands, and the choices we make will determine our future.

Spirituality as a Basis for the Coming Worldshift

Introduction to Round Seven

Is there a role for spirituality in a time of crisis? Can it be of help in facing and eventually overcoming the crisis?

The answer, given in the four stupendous contributions to this final round of the book, is a resounding yes. The present crisis contains both danger and opportunity. The danger is that the systems that drive our world take us to a point of no return where the world collapses around us, and the opportunity is a chance to change the dynamic of the systems so they take us toward a world that is more equitable, sustainable, and peaceful. To achieve this "worldshift" we need both dependable information and deep insight: the former from science and the latter from spirituality. We can't make it without either of them, but with both, we have a chance.

Gregg Braden and Bruce Lipton diagnose the nature of the crisis in which we find ourselves and highlight the nature of the insights we need to cope with it. Joanna Macy and Duane Elgin offer specific advice regarding the insights and the practices we need to face the crisis. Together they paint a concise yet clear and trenchant image of what is wrong with the world and how we could change our thinking and actions to right it.

When writing is as clear and pertinent as this, there is no need to comment further. We cannot point to one or another element of information and the advice it conveys: we would need to point to all of them. But there is no need to cite the whole of these worldshifting papers, for they can be read and reread here—and taken to heart and to mind so they can inspire our hearts and inform our minds. With inspiration coming from the great spiritual traditions and information from the leading edge of the sciences, we can empower ourselves to change, both profoundly and urgently. Then we have a chance to change the world.

The world needs to change, profoundly and urgently, and we are being called forth to take responsibility and assist in this critical worldshift.

25

Deep Wisdom

The Marriage of Science and Spirituality

GREGG BRADEN

During the last years of the cold war, I had a front row seat as a senior systems designer in the defense industry to one of the most frightening times in the history of the world and the thinking that led to it. During the last years of the most potentially lethal, yet undeclared, war in human history, the superpowers of the United States and the former Soviet Union did something that seems unthinkable to any rationally minded person today. They spent the time, energy, and human resources to develop and stockpile somewhere in the neighborhood of sixty-five thousand nuclear weapons—a combined arsenal with the power to microwave Earth, and everything on it, many times over.

The rationale for such an extreme effort stems from a way of thinking that has dominated much of the modern world for the last three hundred years or so, since the beginning of the scientific era. It's based in the false assumptions of scientific thinking that suggest we're somehow separate from the planet Earth and separate from one another and that the nature that gives us life is based on relentless struggle and survival of the strongest. Fortunately, new discoveries have revealed that each of these assumptions is absolutely false. Unfortunately, however, there is a reluctance to reflect such new discoveries in the mainstream media, traditional classrooms, and conventional textbooks. In other words, we're still teaching our young people the false assumptions of an obsolete way of thinking based on struggle, competition, and war.

While we no longer face the nuclear threat that we did in the 1980s, the thinking that made the cold war possible is still in place. This fact is vital to us all right now for one simple reason: for the first time in human history the future of our entire species rests on the choices of a single generation—us—and the choices are being made within a small window of time—now. The best minds of our time are telling us that we must act quickly to avert the clear and present danger of a host of new crises that are converging in a bottleneck of time covering the first years of the twenty-first century.

The journal *Scientific American* released a special edition* to bring the world up to speed on the critical situation we find ourselves in today. The title, "Crossroads for Planet Earth," says it all. The way we solve the simultaneous crises—such as our response to climate change, the unsustainable and growing levels of extreme poverty, the emergence of new diseases, the growing shortages of food and fresh drinking water, the growing chasm between extreme wealth and extreme poverty, and the unsustainable demand for energy—will chart the destiny or seal the fate of our global family, which is estimated to reach a staggering eight billion by 2025.

The key here is that the way we address the greatest crises of human history is based on the way we think of ourselves and the world. Clearly, the thinking that led to the wars and suffering of the twentieth century is not the thinking on which we want the delicate choices of our survival based!

Developing a new level of thinking is precisely what we need to do today, and the magnitude of the crises that face us may prove to be the

---

*The special edition was volume 293, number 3, dated September 2005.

catalyst for doing just that! The emerging bridge between the sciences that tell us how the universe works and the spiritual traditions that give knowledge and meaning to our lives plays a vital role in the new thinking that heads off the darkest possibilities of our future. But while the crises of the moment may be the catalyst for such a shift in thinking, something even deeper is emerging.

The new shift in thinking is the gateway to human transformation. And because of the sheer number of people involved in the shift and the growing magnitude of the crises that are driving us to change the way we think, we are standing on the threshold of human transformation at a level unlike anything ever before known on Earth.

The spiritual traditions that I'm describing are the core principles of ancient and time-tested understandings—principles now confirmed by twentieth-century science that include the interconnected nature of all things, the power of the human heart to positively influence the magnetic fields of Earth and all life, and the cyclic nature of life, climate, civilization, and change. In their spiritual traditions, our ancestors got these principles right, and they embodied them at the core of their lives in their time. It's the marriage of these holistic principles with the best science of today that helps us to tip the scales of life, balance, and peace in our favor.

While the specifics of spiritual principles may vary from tradition to tradition, the essence of their message does not. It's simple, direct, and states that we live in a world where everything has meaning and is meaningful to everything else. What happens in the oceans has meaning for the climate of the mountains. What happens in a river has meaning for the life that depends on the river. The choices that you and I make as we express our beliefs in our living rooms and around family dinner tables have meaning for the people in our immediate lives as well as for those connected through the coherence fields of the human heart living halfway around the planet.

By crossing the traditional boundaries that define science, religion, and the history of our past, we are shown the power of a larger, integrated, and holistic worldview. I cannot help but believe that our destiny and fate as a species are intimately entwined with our willingness to accept the deep wisdom of a spiritually based science. It's all about the way we think of our relationship to Earth, and our relationship to one another, and ourselves. When the facts become clear, our choices become obvious.

26

The Role of Spirituality
in a Worldshift

BRUCE LIPTON

We are truly living in exciting times. The challenges and crises facing the world today are portents of imminent change in civilization. We are on the threshold of an incredible global evolutionary shift.

The current panoply of global crises reveals we are facing our own extinction. Scientists acknowledge that the current degradation of the environment and the massive loss of species are evidence that we are deep into the sixth mass extinction to hit Earth since the origin of life. Unlike the first five massive die-offs, which are attributed to physical causes such as life-destroying geological upheavals and the impact of comets and asteroids, the current wave of extinctions is due to a source much closer to home: human behavior. Our way of life is wreaking havoc in the global community, and our survival is now in question.

Crises are harbingers of evolution. Albert Einstein wisely proffered, "We can't solve problems by using the same kind of thinking we used when we created them." Consequently, the planet's hope and salvation lie in the adoption of the revolutionary new knowledge being revealed at the frontiers of science. This new awareness is shattering old myths and rewriting the truths that shape the character of human civilization.

This new science revises four fundamental beliefs that have shaped civilization. These flawed assumptions include (1) the Newtonian vision of the primacy of a physical, mechanical universe, (2) the belief that genes control biology, (3) the belief that evolution resulted from random genetic mutations, and (4) the belief that evolution is driven by a struggle for the survival of the fittest. These failed beliefs represent the "four assumptions of the apocalypse," for they are driving human civilization to the brink of extinction.

Modern science is predicated on truths verified through accurate observation and measurements of physical world phenomena. Science ignores the spiritual realm because it is not amenable to scientific analysis. As importantly, the predictive success of Newtonian theory, emphasizing the primacy of a physical universe, made the existence of spirit and God an extraneous hypothesis that offered no explanatory principles needed by science.

In the wake of Newtonian theory, with the hand of God out of the way, society has been preoccupied with dominating and controlling nature. Charles Darwin's theory further exacerbates the situation by suggesting that humans evolved through the happenstance of random genetic mutations. Accordingly, we evolved by pure chance, which by extension means without an underlying purpose for our existence. Darwinian theory removed the last link between God, spirit, and the human experience.

Additionally, Darwinism emphasizes that evolution is based on the survival of the fittest in the struggle for existence. For science, the end of the evolutionary struggle is simply represented by survival. As for the means to that end, apparently anything goes. Darwinism leaves humanity without a moral compass.

A mechanical, Newtonian universe in combination with Darwin's theory of random evolution disconnects us from nature and spirit while legitimizing the exploitation and degradation of our fellow humans and the environment. Modern science has led the world to shift from spiritual aspirations to a war for material accumulation. In addition to terrorizing the world's human population, scientific progress has terrorized Mother Nature herself. Our credo, "better living through chemistry," has led to our efforts to control nature with toxic petrochemicals. As a result, we have polluted the environment, undermined the harmony of the biosphere, and are rapidly driving ourselves toward extinction.

All is not lost. Advances from science's frontier offer new insights that provide a bright light at the end of this dark tunnel. For example, in contrast with the emphasis on the Newtonian material realm, the newer science of quantum mechanics reveals that the universe and all of its physical matter are actually made out of immaterial energy. Atoms are not physical particles; they are made of energy vortices resembling nano-tornadoes.

Quantum physics stresses that the invisible energy realm, collectively referred to as the field, is the primary governing force of the material realm. It is more than interesting that the term *field* is defined as "invisible moving forces that influence the physical realm," for the same definition is used to describe the term *spirit*. The new physics provides a modern version of ancient spirituality. In a universe made out of energy, everything is entangled and everything is one.

Biomedical research has recently toppled the widespread belief that organisms are genetically controlled robots and that evolution is driven by a random, survival-of-the-fittest mechanism. As genetically controlled "robots," we are led to perceive of ourselves as victims of heredity. Genes control our lives, yet we did not pick our genes, nor can we change them if we don't like our traits. The perception of genetic victimization inevitably leads to irresponsibility, for we believe we have no power over our lives.

The exciting new science of epigenetics emphasizes that genes are controlled by the environment and, more importantly, by our perception of the environment. Epigenetics acknowledges that we are not victims, but masters, for we can change our environment or perceptions and create up to thirty thousand variations for each of our genes.

Quantum physics and epigenetics provide amazing insight into the mystery of the mind-body-spirit connection. While Newtonian physics and genetic theory dismiss the power of our minds, the new science recognizes that consciousness endows us with powerful creative abilities to shape our lives and the world in which we live. Our thoughts, attitudes, and beliefs control behavior, regulate gene expression, and provide for our life experiences.

In contrast with random mutations, science has identified adaptive mutation mechanisms, wherein organisms adjust their genetics to conform to existing environmental conditions. We did not get here by chance. Every new organism introduced into the biosphere supported harmony and balance in the garden. Every organism is intimately engaged with the environment in a delicate pas de deux. Human existence is not a random accident, but a carefully choreographed event that takes into account the cooperative nature of the biosphere. Humans evolved as the most powerful force in supporting nature's vitality. However, we have misused that power and are now paying the price for our destructive behavior.

The crises we face present us with the greatest opportunity in human history—conscious evolution. Through consciousness, our minds have the power to change our planet and ourselves. It is time we heed the wisdom of the ancient indigenous people and channel our consciousness and spirit to tend the garden and not destroy it.

The story of human life on Earth is yet to be determined. Our evolution depends on whether we are willing to make changes in our individual and collective beliefs and behaviors and whether we are able to make these changes in time. The good news is that biology and evolution are on our side. Evolution—like heaven—is not a destination, but a practice.

A miraculous healing awaits this planet once we accept our new responsibility to collectively tend the garden. When a critical mass of people truly own this belief in their hearts and minds and begin living from these truths, our world will emerge from the darkness in what will amount to a consciousness-based worldshift—a spontaneous evolution for humans, by humans.

27

Worldshift

Learning to Live in a Living Universe

DUANE ELGIN

The most fundamental question facing humanity is, At its foundations, is the universe dead or alive? In short, was Plato correct when, more than two thousand years ago, he said, "The universe is a single living creature that encompasses all living creatures within it"?

We can begin to answer this question by turning to both science and the world's wisdom traditions. Science now regards our universe as (1) almost entirely invisible (with 96 percent of the known universe composed of invisible energy and matter), (2) completely unified and able to communicate with itself instantaneously in ways that transcend the limits of the speed of light, (3) sustained by the flow-through of an unimaginably vast amount of energy, and (4) having freedom at its deepest, quantum levels. While not proving the universe is alive, these and other attributes from science do point strongly in that direction.

When we turn to the world's wisdom traditions and ask how they regard the universe, we find in the words of their followers a stunning consensus that the universe is a continuously regenerated, living presence.

> *God is creating the entire universe, fully and totally, in this present now. Everything God created . . . God creates now all at once.*
>
> MEISTER ECKHART, CHRISTIAN MYSTIC

> *My solemn proclamation is that a new universe is created every moment.*
>
> D. T. SUZUKI, ZEN TEACHER

> *The Tao is the sustaining Life-force and the mother of all things; from it, all things rise and fall without cease.*
>
> LAO-TZU, *TAO TE CHING* (TAOISM)

> *God keeps a firm hold on heavens and earth, preventing them from vanishing away.*
>
> QUR'AN (ISLAM)

> *Evolution presupposes creation . . . creation is an everlasting process—a creation continua.*
>
> POPE JOHN PAUL II

These quotes just begin to describe the profound aliveness of the universe as seen through the lens of the world's wisdom traditions.

What difference does it make if the universe is dead or alive at its foundations? When children are starving, the climate is destabilizing, oil is dwindling, and the population is growing, why is it important to put our attention here? The following sections cover just a few of the reasons why aliveness makes a profound difference.

CONSUMERISM OR SIMPLICITY?

Materialism is a rational response to living in a dead universe. In a material universe, consumerism offers a source of identity and a measure of significance and accomplishment. Where do I find pleasure in a nonliving universe? In things. How do I know that I amount to anything? By how much stuff I have accumulated. How should I relate to the world? By exploiting that which is dead on behalf of the living. Consumerism and exploitation are natural outcomes of a dead-universe perspective. However, if we view the foundations of the universe as being intensely alive, then it makes sense to minimize the material clutter and needless busy-ness and develop the areas where we feel most alive—nurturing relationships, caring communities, creative expressions, time in nature, and service to others.

INDIFFERENT OR WELCOMING?

If we regard the universe as dead at its foundations, then feelings of existential alienation, anxiety, dread, and fear are understandable. Why seek communion with the cold indifference of lifeless matter and empty space? If we relax, we will simply sink into existential despair. However, if we live in a living universe, then feelings of subtle connection, curiosity, and gratitude are understandable. We see ourselves as participants in a cosmic garden of life that has been patiently developing over billions of years. A living-universe perspective invites us to shift from indifference, fear, and cynicism to curiosity, love, and awe.

BIOLOGICAL OR BIO-COSMIC?

Are we no more than a bundle of chemical and neurological interactions? If so, the boundaries of our being are defined by the extent of our physical body. However, in a living universe, our physical existence is permeated and sustained by an aliveness that is inseparable from the larger universe. Seeing ourselves as part of the unbroken fabric of creation awakens our sense of connection with, and compassion for, the totality of life. We recognize our bodies as precious, biodegradable vehicles for acquiring ever deepening experiences of aliveness.

SEPARATE OR INTERCONNECTED?

If we are no more than biological entities, then it makes sense to see ourselves as disconnected from the suffering of other living beings. However, if we are all swimming in the same ocean of subtle aliveness, then it makes sense that we would each have a direct experience of communion with, and concern for, the well-being of others. If we share the same matrix of existence, then the rest of life is already touching both me and you and cocreating the field of aliveness within which we exist.

PULL APART OR PULL TOGETHER?

If we see the universe as mostly barren and devoid of life, then it is natural to see our time on Earth as primarily a struggle for material existence. In turn, it makes sense that we humans would pull apart in conflict. However, if we see the universe as intensely alive and our journey here as one of discovery and learning, then it makes sense that we would pull together in cooperation in order to realize this magnificent potential.

Our view of the universe as either dead or alive creates the context within which we understand who we are and where we are going. In turn, it is vitally important that we have an accurate understanding of our cosmic home. Where a dead-universe perspective generates alienation, environmental destruction, and despair, a living-universe perspective generates feelings of communion, stewardship, and the promise of a higher pathway for humanity. Although the idea of a living universe has ancient roots in human experience, it is now radically new as the frontiers of modern science cut away superstition and reveal the authentic mystery, subtlety, and aliveness of our cosmic home.

28

Spiritual Practices for This Time of Crisis

JOANNA MACY

At this turning in humanity's journey, science and spirituality converge, and we can glimpse new possibilities for a life-sustaining civilization. But the going is rough. One megadisaster follows another. Economic, political, and ecological systems spin out of control in what David Korten aptly calls the great unraveling.

As the rug is progressively pulled out from under us, it is easy to panic, and even easier to simply shut down. These two instinctive reactions—panic and paralysis—are the roadside ditches that border our pathway to a livable future. To fall into either one is the greatest of all the dangers we face, for they deaden the heart and derail the mind. If ever we needed spiritual practices and disciplines for staying alert and connected, it is now.

The greatest gift we can give our world is our presence, awake and attentive. What can help us do that? Here, drawn from ancient religions and Earth wisdom traditions, are a handful of practices I have learned to count on.

BREATHE

Our friend the breath is always with us. When we pay attention to its flow, it merges mind with body and connects inner world with outer world. Mindfulness of breathing in and breathing out can center and steady you.

"Feel how your breathing makes more space around you," writes the poet Rainer Maria Rilke. "Pure, continuous exchange with all that is, flow and counterflow where rhythmically we come to be."

Notice that you are not deciding each time to exhale or inhale; it's rather that you're being breathed. Breathed by life. And so are all the other animals, and plants too, in vast rhythms of reciprocity. Feel that web enlivening you and holding you.

The felt flow-through of matter and/or energy brings a measure of ease and opens us to the flow-through of information as well. This lowers our usual defenses against distressing information and begins to unblock the feedback loops so we can more clearly perceive what we've caused to happen.

COME FROM GRATITUDE

As burning rain forests and dying plankton progressively diminish our oxygen supply, each breath seems more precious. Thankfulness for that precious gift galvanizes us to act, to protect.

With gratitude we affirm our birthright to be here in Earth, endowed with self-reflexive consciousness, the power to choose. To be here in solidarity with each other. To be a living, intrinsic, blessed part of this living Earth.

We have excellent teachers of gratitude in indigenous peoples the world over, and especially Native Americans. In every council meeting of the Six Nation confederacy of the Haudenosaunee, the thanksgiving address constitutes "the words that come before all else." Spoken afresh each time with spontaneous variations, these words offer not only thanks but also greetings to each being and element of the natural world they honor. I think this practice is at the root of the dignity and self-respect that has survived centuries of dispossession and humiliation.

As we adapt this practice to our own lives, say at the start and close of each day, and even bring it into meetings, we make two discoveries. The first is that gratitude is not dependent on external circumstances. The second is that gratitude is a revolutionary act. Helping us realize how much we already have, it helps to free us from the grip of the consumer society.

RESPECT YOUR PAIN FOR THE WORLD

We are in grief. With all that's being inflicted on the natural world and the social fabric of our lives together, there's fear too, anger as well. These responses are natural and healthy. If we disown them, we cripple our vitality and intelligence.

So we bow to them instead. When pain for the world arises within you, recognize it and pause. Pause and breathe, as if making room for it, as if letting that pain flow through your heart. Realize that you are capable of suffering with your world. "Suffering with" is the literal meaning of the word *compassion*. It is proof positive of our interconnectedness, indeed of our inescapable interexistence.

"There is no birth of consciousness without pain," said Carl Gustav Jung. Our pain for the world releases us from the illusion of separation. It has a key role to play in birthing the collective consciousness that may well be the only resolution to the global crisis of our time.

ENGAGE THE POWER OF BENEVOLENCE

Metta, or loving kindness, is a Buddhist meditation-in-action that many today are finding wonderfully efficacious. It is good for dispelling fear and ill will as well as for generating care and understanding.

This practice functions not as a vague, diaphanous feeling, but as a series of fairly precise person-by-person intentions. One traditional Burmese practice, for example, takes a fourfold form, such as this:

> May (a specific person) be free from physical suffering.
> May he or she be free from mental suffering.
> May he or she be free from conflict.
> May he or she have ease of well-being.

It's important to extend this to oneself as well (May I be free from mental suffering, and so on). Variations are encouraged (May he or she be free to develop the beauty of his or her mind.) This practice, when in play, cannot coexist with fear.

INHABIT LARGER FIELDS OF TIME

We are relating to time today in a way that is surely unique in human history. The growth economy and nano-technologies require decisions made at lightning speed for short-term goals, cutting us off from nature's rhythms and from the past and future as well. Both the legacy of our ancestors and the needs of our descendants become less and less real to us.

This relationship to time is not innate. Throughout history men and women have labored at great personal cost to bequeath to future generations monuments of art and learning they would not see completed in their lifetimes. And they honored through story and ritual those who came before.

We, too, can broaden the temporal context of our lives. To help us do that, cosmology and evolutionary sciences now offer vast vistas into the past. As to connecting with the future, ten thousand generations are now brought within our reach by nuclear wastes. The consequences of our actions (our karma) play out on a geological time scale.

Our moral imagination is the essential tool for opening us up to the depths and breadths of time to which we belong. Extend it both backward and forward. Open your mind's eye to the immense journey of life on our planet by meditating on your hand. "See" its evolutionary development, one life-form to another, from its origins as a fin in primordial seas. Behold in it also the countless generations of human hands whose tasks and skills shaped our world.

Invite the future ones into your awareness. Feel the strength of your desire that they find clean air to breathe, water to drink, trees, topsoil. Try asking for their guidance in the work that is now to be done. And—for a practice I hope you'll enjoy as much as I have—imagine a person of a century or two hence (perhaps related to you, perhaps not) who can see back through time and sees you at this moment of your life. Now write yourself a letter from this future being.

Afterword

A Call for Change—
Fostering an Effective Worldshift

ERVIN LASZLO
AND KINGSLEY L. DENNIS

The twenty-eight profound and inspiring essays that make up this unique volume have provided more than enough food for thought. They have offered us a diverse, we may even say nutritious, menu on which to slowly digest and reflect. We hope that the reader has been provoked, inspired—even prodded perhaps—into new avenues of thought and inquiry. At the very least we hope that these essays have stimulated further inquiry, investigation, and discussion.

Before we leave the reader, we wish to offer our own thoughts on the present condition of humanity on this planet. We would like to comment on how two vast and now increasingly diverging systems—those of nature, that is, the biosphere, and the globally interacting human community—are colliding. This is another indication of how our rational scientific minds, dominating our intuitive, spiritually oriented minds, have been at least partly responsible for the divorce of humanity from its natural, living environment.

When we speak of the need for profound and urgent change we should specify that this refers to the system of the human community and not to the system of nature. The biosphere needs to be conserved, its integrity safeguarded, its dynamic equilibria maintained and made more resilient. It is not to be pushed to a tipping point, for the dynamic regime into which it would then settle is not likely to be favorable to the persistence of the human community. After all, the human system has been built into the system of nature during the millennia that have elapsed since the last Ice Age. The human system could persist, and even thrive, because it was in harmony with the generative and regenerative capacities of the biosphere. This was the case in our historical past when our systems of knowledge were imbued with our spiritual gnosis. This was always a delicate harmony that has now gone out of balance because what we have been able to do with our scientific tools has, in most cases, outstripped the reflective processes of our spiritual understanding. We are now a vast system of 7 billion humans, with enormous scientific and technological powers, unprecedented demands, and a partly dysfunctional collective mind-set that is already in transition.

The human/nature system mesh has precious little error tolerance in our day. We are dependent on a proper mesh for obtaining the basic resources of our life: air, water, food, habitable space, and the diverse mineral and biological resources on which we have now come to depend. And we are running out, or at any rate low, on most if not all of these resources.

Let us be very careful, then, about what change we are speaking, and where. In regard to the system of nature, we can speak of safeguarding and maintaining, rebalancing, restabilizing, and making more resilient the current system, but we cannot speak of intervening in it to create change and transformation. Given the limitations of human knowledge, any change we would catalyze would be very likely detrimental to the web of life on Earth, including the ever-more-precarious system of human life.

Precisely the opposite is the case in regard to the human system on the planet. This system, which developed out of an embrace with the nature system, has now overgrown, or rather, shrugged off, that embrace. We have entered on mistaken paths of development and have disregarded their unintended consequences as side effects or collateral damage. When these consequences have become painfully evident, we have resorted to technology and our scientific tools to compensate for the negative effects. And we have continued to grow. We have artificially increased the fertility of soils and tapped energies beyond those that sustain the nature system. We have built enormous urban complexes and used the resources of vast hinterlands to sustain them. These and similar measures have given us the illusion of stability and progress, when in reality they have undermined the vital balances on which our very existence depends.

Now we had better learn to live within the embrace of the nature system, reintegrating ourselves within the limits and possibilities of the processes and equilibria of the biosphere. This requires a radical shift in the human system—a "worldshift."

Current attempts to restabilize or revitalize the dominant structures and processes of the present world are a grievous mistake. Success could only be temporary, and it would only postpone the day of reckoning, making it all the more dramatic, and possibly traumatic. This is because the processes we have initiated in this system cannot be simply stopped—not population growth, not resource consumption, not the progressive degeneration of natural cycles and resources. Yet our political and business leaders speak of restabilizing and revitalizing our ailing social, economic, and environmental systems as the way to solve our problems, erroneously believing that science will come to the rescue in all matters.

The bottom line is that we must change, but we must know *what* to change, and *how*. We know that the future will not be a linear continuation of the past. It will encounter a tipping point—a bifurcation in the evolutionary trajectory of the human system. It is our unique and very likely nonrecurring opportunity to orient the thinking of today's people, especially young people, so they will face the tipping point with a clear recognition that it is our world that needs to change, and change profoundly, while the system that supports life on the planet must be made more stable and resilient so it can enable us to shift our world without a collapse of our population.

Seizing this opportunity calls for realizing that if we are to change the world—*our* world—we must first change ourselves. In other words, we must change the way we look at the world and ourselves—must change our consciousness. This change requires that we realize that a fragmentation between our scientific, rational knowledge and our spiritual, intuitive insight will only lead to an ever increasing dislocation between the human species and its natural life-support systems. An integral and unified understanding is imperative. We are in dire need for "nondual thinking" for fostering an effective *worldshift*.

THE WORLDSHIFT HAS STARTED

More and more people seem convinced that something dramatic will happen at the end of 2012. While the world will not suddenly become a paradise on earth, we could launch a process that would take it in that direction because when the end of 2012 comes and goes, it will be a signal to the world that there very definitely *is* a future awaiting us. Yet what that future will turn out to be is not decided. All we know is that the processes of change that have been building throughout the twentieth century will reach a point of no return—the point at which whatever direction they take will become effectively irreversible. Now, in the spring and summer of 2012, we are on the cusp of that critical tipping point.

We should have long known that the world we have created is not sustainable. In 1962, in her seminal book *Silent Spring,* Rachel Carson told us that the way we treat our environment is not tenable and is bound to backfire, and in 1972 the Club of Rome published *The Limits to Growth,* a book by Donella H. Matthews based on a computerized world model with social and economic as well as ecological parameters. It predicted that in the absence of major change, the world system would collapse in less than a hundred years. Today the condition of unsustainability is widely recognized, but not many realize that we don't have a hundred years before it reaches a tipping point.

We live in a time of crises. The crises are many and diverse, but their cause is basically the same: a serious and, in the absence of determined change, terminal mismanagement of our affairs on this planet. Let us briefly look at some of these issues facing us today.

- ► There is unsustainability in the ecology. The way we withdraw and consume water and manage our productive lands and the resources of the sea cannot be prolonged for long. A growing population with growing per capita resource consumption is rapidly depleting the vital resources of the planet. The way we pollute the air is not sustainable either: it will soon present serious health hazards, especially in urban and industrial agglomerations.

- ► There is unsustainability in the economy. Despite great advances in the technologies of production and distribution, the gap is growing between the rich and the poor. In their search for markets and profits, mainstream businesses feed people's appetite for resource consumption, pushing one natural resource after another past peak production into decline. In its present form the global financial system is entirely untenable, yet bankers and politicians still try to stabilize it.

- ► Social structures are breaking down in countries both developed and developing, and inequality and injustice, exposed by global flows of information, fuel resentment and revolt. Grassroots movements to overthrow dictators and power elites are sweeping Africa and are spreading to Asia and Latin America. Growing waves of migrants move from social and political hot spots and ecologically threatened areas toward relatively stable and prosperous regions, where they stress society and overload the economy and the ecology.

In addition to unsustainabilities of our own creation, nature produces cataclysms of its own. These, as the earthquake off the shores of Japan showed, can create social and technological breakdowns that vastly magnify the disruptions and damages.

Yet living in a crisis-ridden world has its positive side. The silver lining at the edge of the gathering clouds is what the Chinese had long known but we have all but forgotten: crisis is both danger and opportunity. The dangers are now evident, and also the opportunities are becoming visible. A "green economy" offers farsighted entrepreneurs new ways to grow by shifting to less wasteful and hazardous forms of resource production and use. Unpredictable fluctuations prompt more and more people to ask whether today's unstable and inequitable financial system could be replaced with a system where money is used to enhance life and well-being rather than to make more money. The nuclear meltdown in Japan triggered a worldwide debate on whether there is a future based on this inherently dangerous technology. Is "nuclear future" an oxymoron? Do we really need to boil water by fissioning the atom in order to produce steam to drive old-fashioned turbines to generate electricity when we know how to transform a stream of photons into a stream of electrons and can harness the power of wind, water, plants, and tide?

The dangers are real, and they are less and less tolerant of delay. Fortunately the opportunities to create real change are growing as well. In business, in the media, and even in politics, the will to explore alternatives is growing. The rapid rise of investment in clean technologies and green products, the wave of socially and ecologically conscious electoral shifts in Europe as well as in Latin America, and the revolt of the suppressed masses in the Arab countries are signs that people—entire societies—are ready to leave the status quo and set out on new paths. The worldshift is now under way.

Choosing our future by consciously furthering and steering the burgeoning worldshift is the greatest opportunity ever to have been granted a generation in history. It is up to us to seize it and ensure the future of humankind on the planet. In truth, many of us will already be feeling these similar stirrings deep within our hearts. We sense that change is coming and that the inevitable approaches. Something new is happening: a new vision and a new future are coming into being. Yet we have to want to make the change happen.

TO CHANGE OR NOT TO CHANGE— THAT IS *NOT* THE QUESTION

But *how* to change and *what* to change—that *is* the question.

People who are concerned about sustainability in the world know that something has to be done to keep this world going; changes have to be made. But they don't agree on the nature of the changes: some call for far more drastic changes than others. We need to change the structures and processes of the human system, and this change must be fundamental: it needs to be a true worldshift. At the same time change in the system that provides our basic life support must be gradual, incremental, and respectful of the interdependence of its elements and processes. The "worldshifters" need to focus on transforming the human system, and the "stabilizers" on increasing the resilience in the natural system. Clarity on this issue may be a precondition of creating a sustainable future for humankind on the planet. We thus need to turn our attention to the critical role of our current dominant cultures in helping to usher in a global, sustainable future.

The values and associated behaviors of the dominant cultures of the contemporary world gave rise to a globally extended system that is not sustainable in its present form. If a cataclysmic breakdown is to be averted, the influential cultures that have shaped today's world must change. Consciously moving toward a harmonious system of cooperative societies focused on the shared objective of sustaining the systems of life on the planet is an urgent necessity. To this end a mutation is needed in the cultures of the contemporary world, so as to create the values and aspirations that would bring together today's individually diverse and largely self-centered societies in the shared mission of ensuring the sustainability of the systems of life in the biosphere.

The basic fact is that today's world system is highly diverse, but it is insufficiently coordinated. Creating a higher level of unity within its diversity is intrinsically feasible, but this task calls for system-maintaining cooperation among the diverse societies that make up the human world. This shift on the plane of practice is not likely to come about without a corresponding shift in the values and aspirations that govern the nature of practice in the world. Today's socioeconomic and ecological world system is structurally unstable and dynamically unsustainable. This condition has been created by practices oriented by the values and perceptions of a dominant layer of society. These values and perceptions have now become largely obsolete. Consider the following examples.

Nature is inexhaustible. The long-standing belief that Earth is an inexhaustible source of resources and an inexhaustible sink of wastes leads to the overmining of natural resources and overloading of the biosphere's regenerative cycles.

The biosphere is a mechanism. The belief that we can engineer the biosphere like a building or a bridge is producing a plethora of unforeseen and vexing side effects, such as the destruction of natural balances and the disappearance of myriad living species.

Life is a struggle where the fittest survives. This application of Darwin's theory of natural selection to society is mistaken in principle (Darwin did not mean by "fittest" the strongest and most aggressive, but the most adaptive and cooperative), and it is dangerous: it produces a growing gap between the rich and the poor and legitimates the use of force on the premise that the possession of power is the natural attribute of a species that is fit to survive.

The market distributes benefits. The free market, governed by Adam Smith's principle of the "invisible hand," is believed to distribute the benefits of economic activity in society. However, the poverty and marginalization of nearly half of the world's population indicates that under current conditions trust in this belief is unfounded. The invisible hand does not operate: the holders of wealth and power garner for themselves a disproportionate share of the material benefits resulting from economic activity.

Some of the current beliefs produce paradoxical conditions.

- Millions of people are suffering from overeating and obesity, while a thousand million go hungry.
- 6 million children die annually of starvation, and 155 million are overweight.
- There are millions of intelligent women ready to play a responsible role in society, but they don't get a fair chance in education, business, politics, and civic life.
- In order to save on the cost of labor, millions are put out of work, wasting human capital that is essential to tackle the social, economic, and environmental problems now faced by humanity.
- Vast herds of animals are brought into the world for the sole purpose of being slaughtered for meat, something that, apart from its questionable ethical and health implications, is wasting an enormous amount of water and grain (used to feed the animals), resources urgently needed to ensure nutrition for human populations.
- The problems of the human community call for long-term solutions, but the criterion for success in the business world is the bottom line in the annual or semiannual corporate profit-and-loss statements.
- The planet is bathed in solar energy, and technologies are online to tap the energy of wind, tides, hot subsurface rocks, biomass,

and animal waste and by-products, yet the world continues to run on polluting and finite fossil fuels and inherently dangerous nuclear power.

▶ High-tech weapons that are more dangerous than the conflicts they are intended to cope with are developed and stockpiled at vast investment of money and human and natural resources.

▶ The ineffectiveness of military force to achieve economic and political objectives has been demonstrated over and over again, yet the world's governments spend over $1.2 trillion dollars a year on arms, wars, and military establishments and similar amounts on empire-building objectives often disguised as projects of national defense and homeland security.

Such values and beliefs, and the conditions to which they give rise, produce multiple strands and forms of unsustainability. They are manifest in the contemporary world in the spheres of society, the economy, and the ecology. Such principle strands of unsustainability include the following:

Unsustainable conditions in society. In the rich countries job security is disappearing, competition is intensifying, and family life is suffering. More and more men and women find satisfaction and companionship outside rather than within the home. And in the home, many of the functions of family life are atrophying, taken over by outside interest groups. Child rearing is increasingly entrusted to kindergartens and company or community day-care centers. The provision of daily nourishment is shifting from the family kitchen to supermarkets, prepared-food industries, and fast-food chains. Leisure-time activities are colored by the marketing and public relations campaigns of commercial enterprises. Children's media exposure to TV, video games, and "adult" themes is increasing, and it motivates violent and sexually exploitative behavior. Social structures are breaking down in both the rich and the poor countries.

In poor countries the struggle for economic survival destroys the traditional extended family. In some countries destitute children are recruited as soldiers and forced into prostitution or are forced to venture into the streets as beggars.

Unsustainability in the economy. The human community is economically polarized: there is a large and in some regions still growing gap between diverse layers of the population. The gap depresses the quality of life of hundreds of millions of people and reduces the chances of survival of the poorest and most severely marginalized populations.

(i) **Wealth distribution.** Wealth and income differences have reached staggering proportions. The combined wealth of the world's billionaires equals the income of 3 billion people, nearly half of the world's population. Eighty percent of the global domestic product belongs to 1 billion people, and the remaining 20 percent is shared by 6 billion. Poverty has not diminished in absolute numbers. In the poorest countries 78 percent of the urban population subsists under life-threatening circumstances; one in three urban dwellers lives in slums, shantytowns, and urban ghettoes, and nearly 1 billion are classified as slum dwellers. Of the 7 billion people who now share the planet, 1.4 billion subsist on the equivalent of less than $1.25 a day, and an additional 1.6 billion live on less than $2.50 a day.

(ii) **Resource use.** The gap between the rich and the poor shows up in food and energy consumption as well as in the load placed on natural resources. People in North America, Western Europe, and Japan consume 140 percent of their daily caloric requirement, while populations in countries such as Madagascar, Guyana, and Laos live on 70 percent. The average amount of commercial electrical energy consumed by Africans is half a kilowatt-hour (kWh) per person; the corresponding average for Asians and Latin Americans is 2 to

3 kWh, and for Americans, Europeans, Australians, and Japanese, it is 8 kWh. The average American burns five tons of fossil fuel per year, in contrast with the 2.9 tons of the average German, and places twice the environmental load of the average Swede on the planet, three times that of the Italian, thirteen times the Brazilian, thirty-five times the Indian, and two hundred and eighty times the Haitian. Today, for the first time in history, in regard to a number of natural resources, the rising curve of human demand exceeds the descending curve of natural supply. Since the end of World War II, more of the planet's resources have been consumed than in all of history until then. Global consumption is nearing, and in some cases has already surpassed, planetary maxima.

(iii) The financial system. The precarious structure of the world's financial system is a major factor in the unsustainability of the world's economy. Instability in the financial sector is not a new phenomenon, but it was not widely recognized prior to the credit crunch of 2008. The bubble that burst at that time has led to the loss of over 2 million jobs in the United States alone and resulted in a global reduction of wealth estimated at 2.8 trillion dollars. The structural unsustainability of the world's financial system is not uniquely due to the creation and bursting of speculative bubbles: it is rooted in the imbalance of international trade. Already in 2005, the International Monetary Fund's *Economic Outlook* report noted that it is no longer a question of *whether* the world's economies will adjust, only *how* they will adjust. If measures are further delayed, the adjustment could be "abrupt," with hazardous consequences for global trade, economic development, and international security.

Unsustainability in the ecology. Social, economic, and financial unsustainability is exacerbated by damages produced by human activity in the environment, resulting in a diminution of the resources effectively available for social and industrial use.

(i) Water. The amount of water available for per capita consumption is diminishing. In 1950 there was a potential reserve of nearly 17,000 cubic meters of fresh water for every person then living. Since then the rate of water withdrawal has been more than double the rate of population growth, and in consequence in 1999 the per capita world water reserves decreased to 7,300 cubic meters per person. Today about one-third of the world's population doesn't have access to adequate supplies of clean water, and by 2025 two-thirds of the population will live under conditions of critical water scarcity. By then there may be only 4,800 cubic meters of water reserves per person.

(ii) Productive land. There is a progressive loss of productive land. The Food and Agriculture Organization estimates that there are 7,490 million acres of high-quality cropland available globally, 71 percent of it in the developing world. This quantity is decreasing due to soil erosion, destructuring, compaction, impoverishment, excessive desiccation, accumulation of toxic salts, leaching of nutritious elements, and inorganic and organic pollution caused by urban and industrial wastes. Worldwide, 12 to 17 million acres of cropland are lost per year. At this rate 741 million acres will be lost by midcentury, leaving 6.67 billion acres to support 8 to 9 billion people. (This figure may still be overly optimistic since the amount of available land will be further reduced by flooding due to a progressive rise in sea levels.) The remaining 0.74 acres of productive land will only produce food at the bare subsistence level.

(iii) Air quality. Changes in the chemical composition of the atmosphere have reduced the availability of air capable of supporting adequate health levels. Since the middle of the nineteenth century the oxygen level in the air has decreased, mainly due to the burning of coal, and it now dips to 19 percent of total volume over impacted areas and 12–17 percent over major cities. At 6–7 percent of total volume, life can no longer be sustained. At the same time, the share of greenhouse gases is growing. Two hundred years of burning fossil fuels and cutting down large tracts of forest have increased the atmosphere's carbon dioxide content from about 280 parts per million to over 350 parts per million.

(iv) Climate Change. Conservative elements claim that global climate change is due primarily to natural causes and at the most only exacerbated by human activity: they maintain that a new cycle in the fusion processes that generate heat in the sun is sending an increasing amount of solar radiation to Earth, and this heats up the atmosphere. Climate models show that even relatively minor changes in the composition of the atmosphere can produce major effects, including widespread harvest failures, water shortages, increased spread of diseases, the rise of the sea level, and the die-off of large tracts of forest. Global climate change is already producing persistent drought in various parts of the world. In northern China, for example, prolonged aridity has prompted the government to generate rainfall through artificial cloud seeding. By reducing the yield of productive lands, drought is creating a global food shortage. It is exacerbated by falling world food reserves: the current stocks are not sufficient to cover the needs of the newly food-deficient countries.

The practices that characterize human activity have their roots in the dominant values and perceptions of people. These values and perceptions are now obsolete. Allowing them to inspire action is strongly counterproductive; it produces growing crises and could result in a world-scale breakdown. The values and practices that inspire the dominant practices of the contemporary world need to change. We need a conscious and well-focused cultural mutation. The needed cultural mutation does not require people and societies to reject and discard their cultural heritage or disown their cultural preferences. It only requires a positive change in regard to those values and beliefs that reduce the sustainability of the system that frames human life on the planet.

GROUND RULE FOR HARMONIZING THE DIVERSITY OF THE CONTEMPORARY WORLD

The ground rule for achieving a higher level of unity in the contemporary world is simple and basic: maintain the diversity of the cultures and societies that compose the system, but join it with a higher level of harmony among them. A global-level harmonization of the system's diverse elements would allow the pursuit of a variety of goals and objectives as long as they do not damage those vital balances and processes that maintain the whole system. Achieving a higher level of dynamic stability in the world system is in the best interest of all people and societies since without an adequate level of viability in the whole system, the viability of its parts is compromised.

The basic ground rule is both simple and evident: allow diversity to flourish among the cultures and societies that make up the contemporary socioeconomic and ecological world system, but do not allow this diversity to damage or destroy the harmony required to ensure the overall system's viability.

Additional precepts are required to ensure the effective application of the basic rule.

- ▸ Every society has an equal right to access and use the resources of the planet, but it also has an equal responsibility to sustain the world system on the planet.
- ▸ Every society is free to live in accordance with the values and beliefs that accord with its historical heritage and its current wisdom, as long as these values and beliefs do not result in action that constrains the freedom of other societies to live in accordance with their own values and beliefs.

- ► All societies have a legitimate obligation to safeguard the freedom, physical security, and territorial integrity of their population and to this end maintain an armed force, but no society has the right to produce and stockpile weapons that threaten the freedom, physical security, and territorial integrity of any other society.
- ► All societies have a responsibility to forego technologies that waste essential resources, produce dangerous levels of pollution, or pose a threat to the health and well-being of their own people and the people of other societies.

Embracing these and related ground rules would allow the world system to achieve the unity required to balance its diversity and thereby create and sustain conditions necessary to ensure the flowering of human life and well-being. Motivating and promoting the cultural mutation that would inspire and motivate this vital development is the moral obligation of all conscious and rational members of the human family.

To sum up our "call for change," what we are desperately in need of for fostering an effective worldshift is new thinking. Albert Einstein told us that we can't solve a problem with the same kind of thinking that gave rise to the problem, so if our problem is the obsolescence of the world we have created, we need to shift to a new paradigm for our life and civilization. The same thinking that got us here will bring us to the critical tipping point and to the irreversible leap, which is then likely to be down, rather than up. However, it is our firm conviction that by fostering nondual thinking we will be contributing toward a new paradigm approach that encourages communication, collaboration, and connection. Further, by creating the groundwork for an integral and equitable worldview we will be taking a necessary step on the way to a harmonious and favorable future for humankind on planet Earth.

WorldShift International
A Global Conscious Evolution Initiative

WorldShift International (WSI) is an autonomous worldshift initiative that seeks to promote, support, and engage with the concept of a worldshift within our current global systems as well as an inner worldshift at a personal level and an evolutionary shift in human consciousness.

The WorldShift International website is a portal to information that supports and encourages both an inner-world and external-world shift and aims to provide resources that will help to empower individuals in their own processes and to stimulate an awareness for the urgent need for global change. WorldShift International also hosts the WorldShift Now! social network, inviting individuals to create, develop, and share their own networks of worldshift-aligned interests and activities with like-minded people.

WSI offers a platform on which it invites collaboration with like-minded individuals, groups, and organizations for cultural, political, social, environmental, ecological, and economic reform and for the establishment of a healthy, functional, and progressive global society.

WSI views as imperative the need for us all to recognize the urgent necessity for global change, not only change in our external systems, behaviors, and practices but also change in our very way of thinking. A new consciousness is now required if we are to successfully manage our shift forward into the twenty-first century. It is imperative that we seek the means to transcend the current system and to establish and nurture ways that allow us to live in creative harmony and balance with ourselves, with others, and with nature. As Buckminster Fuller said, *"You never change anything by fighting the existing reality. To change something, build a new model that makes the existing model obsolete."*

WSI is committed to supporting and cocreating a positive, evolutionary change, and it acknowledges the fundamental strength, dignity, resilience, and spirit of each individual and the inherent capacity we all have to make this *shift*.

Find out more by visiting the WSI website: www.worldshiftinternational.org.

WorldShift International: A conscious evolution initiative seeking to ensure that our generation is not the last generation, but the first generation cocreating a new paradigm in which social, cultural, political, and conscious evolutions form the foundations of a harmonious global society.

Contributors

José Argüelles (January 24, 1939–March 23, 2011) was a world-renowned author, artist, visionary, and educator. He was the founder of Planet Art Network and the Foundation for the Law of Time. He held a Ph.D. in art history and aesthetics from the University of Chicago and taught at numerous colleges, including Princeton University and the San Francisco Art Institute. As one of the originators of the Earth Day concept, he founded the first Whole Earth Festival in 1970, at Davis, California, and he was known for his role in organizing the Harmonic Convergence event of 1987. His book *The Mayan Factor: Path Beyond Technology* was published the same year.

Michael Beckwith is a world leader and teacher in the new thought–ancient wisdom tradition of spirituality. He is the founder of the Agape International Spiritual Center and cofounder of the Association for Global New Thought and the Season for Nonviolence, which are extensions of his vision of one human family united on a foundation of peace, based on the spiritual origin of every man, woman, and child. He teaches meditation and scientific prayer and speaks at conferences and seminars and is the originator of the Life Visioning Process and author of *Inspirations of the Heart, 40 Day Mind Fast Soul Feast, A Manifesto of Peace,* and *Living from the Overflow.*

Gregg Braden is a *New York Times* bestselling author, a former senior computer systems designer for Martin Marietta Aerospace, a former computer geologist for Phillips Petroleum, and the first technical operations manager for Cisco Systems. For over twenty-five years he has searched high mountain villages, remote monasteries, and forgotten texts to bridge their life-giving secrets with the best science of today. His work has led to cutting-edge books such as *The Divine Matrix, The Spontaneous Healing of Belief, Fractal Time, and Deep Truth* (published in the fall of 2011). His work is now published in seventeen languages and thirty-three countries and shows beyond any reasonable doubt that the key to our future lies in the wisdom of our past. For more information, visit his website: **www.greggbraden.com**.

Deepak Chopra, M.D., is a world-renowned authority in the field of mind-body healing, a bestselling author, and the founder of the Chopra Center for Wellbeing. Before establishing the Chopra Center, he served as chief of staff at Boston Regional Medical Center. He received his medical degree from the All India Institute of Medical Sciences. Dr. Chopra is the prolific author of more than fifty-five books, including fourteen bestsellers on mind-body health, quantum mechanics, spirituality, and peace. Dr. Chopra's books have been published in more than eighty-five languages.

Kingsley L. Dennis, Ph.D., is a sociologist and writer. He worked as a lecturer in the Sociology Department at Lancaster University (in the United Kingdom) and was a research associate within the Centre for Mobilities Research. He coauthored *After the Car* (2009), which examines post–peak oil societies and mobility, and is the author of *New Consciousness for a New World* (2011) and *The Struggle for Your Mind: Conscious Evolution and the Battle to Control How We Think* (2012). He is also a cofounder of WorldShift International. He currently lives in Andalusia, southern Spain.

Larry Dossey, M.D., is a distinguished Texas physician, deeply rooted in the scientific world, who has become an internationally influential advocate of the role of the mind in health and the role of spirituality in health care. Bringing the experience of a practicing internist and the soul of a poet to the discourse, Dr. Dossey offers panoramic insight into the nature and the future of medicine. The author of nine books and numerous articles, Dr. Dossey is the former executive editor of the peer-reviewed journal *Alternative Therapies in Health and Medicine,* the most widely subscribed-to journal in its field. Dr. Dossey's ever deepening explication of the nonlocal mind provides a legitimate foundation for the merging of spirit and medicine.

Duane Elgin is an author, speaker, educator, consultant, and media activist. For more than three decades, he has defined the cutting edge in consciousness research, in the ecology movement, and in future studies. Elgin has worked as a senior social scientist with the think tank SRI International, where he coauthored numerous studies on the long-range future for government agencies such as the National Science Foundation. He pioneered the voluntary simplicity movement with his now-classic first book, titled by the same name and published in the 1980s. Elgin is the author of several other books, including *Awakening Earth: Exploring the Evolution of Human Culture and Consciousness* (1993) *and Promise Ahead: A Vision of Hope and Action for Humanity's Future* (2000).

Ede Frecska, M.D., is Chief of Department at the National Institute of Psychiatry and Neurology in Budapest, Hungary. He received his medical degree in 1977 from Semmelweis University in Budapest. He then earned qualifications as a certified psychologist from the Department of Psychology at Lorand Eotvos University in Budapest. Dr. Frecska completed his residency training in psychiatry, both in Hungary (1986) and in the United States (1992). He is a qualified psychopharmacologist (1987) of international merit, with fifteen years of clinical and research experience in the United States. In his recent research he is engaged in studies on psychointegrator drugs and techniques, and his theoretical work focuses on the interface between cognitive neuroscience and quantum brain dynamics. He is specifically interested in the mechanism of initiation ceremonies and healing rituals.

Jagdish Gandhi is a visionary and a far-sighted person who has been building bridges of peace across the globe for nearly fifty years. For his long-standing contributions to education in peace, the United Nations awarded the prestigious UNESCO Prize for Peace Education in 2002 to his unique creation, the City Montessori School, popularly known as CMS, which Gandhi founded in 1959 and has served as its founder-manager. He lives simply in the same room in which he began his work for peace in 1959, and he has chosen to have no personal wealth of his own, spending instead all his created resources on his mission. Believing that children are the world's future, he maintains that the best way to mold the future is to nurture it. Persuaded by the UNESCO Constitution that wars begin in the minds of men, he felt it best to build the defenses of peace in the minds of men through education and by nurturing young minds.

Amit Goswami, Ph.D., is professor emeritus in the Physics Department of the University of Oregon, in Eugene, Oregon, where he has served since 1968. He is a pioneer of the new paradigm of science called science within consciousness and the author of the highly successful textbook *Quantum Mechanics.* His two-volume textbook for nonscientists, *The Physicist's View of Nature,* traces the decline and rediscovery of the concept of God within science. He has also written eight popular books based on his research on quantum physics and consciousness. In his seminal book, *The Self-Aware Universe,* he solved the quantum measurement problem elucidating the famous observer effect while paving the path to a new paradigm of science based on the primacy of consciousness.

Beth Green has been guided by an inner voice and a total devotion to authentic spirituality since her awakening in 1980. She has a phenomenal intuitive gift that guides everything she does, from counseling individuals to leading workshops and to writing books and music. In addition to *Living with Reality,* Green has published four other books, composed and performed on three music CDs, developed dozens of workshops on topics as diverse as sex, spirituality, money, and food, and taught people processes that really help them transform. Green also founded the Stream, a spiritual community, in 1983; the spiritual activist movement, which was recently relaunched; and LifeForce, the Inner Workout, an innovative mind-body-spirit exercise program she leads daily for free on the Internet.

Stanislav Grof's professional career has covered a period of more than fifty years in which his primary interest has been research of the heuristic and therapeutic potential of nonordinary states of consciousness. This included initially four years of laboratory research of psychedelics—LSD, psilocybin, mescaline, and tryptamine derivatives, from 1956 to 1960—and fourteen years of research of psychedelic psychotherapy. From 1973 until 1987, he was scholar-in-residence at the Esalen Institute in Big Sur, California, where he developed jointly with his wife, Christina, a powerful nondrug form of self-exploration and psychotherapy that they call holotropic breathwork. They have used this method in workshops and in professional training in North and South America, Europe, Australia, and Asia.

Jean Houston is a scholar, philosopher, and researcher in human capacities and one of the principal founders of the human potential movement. A powerful and dynamic speaker, she holds conferences and seminars with social leaders, educational institutions, and business organizations worldwide. Houston has worked intensively in forty cultures and one hundred countries, helping them to enhance and deepen their own uniqueness while they become part of the global community. Her ability to inspire and invigorate people enables her to readily convey her vision—the finest possible achievement of the individual potential.

Barbara Marx Hubbard is an author, public speaker, social innovator, and president of the Foundation for Conscious Evolution. She has initiated a guided educational program supported by Internet systems called *Gateway to Conscious Evolution*, offering a new developmental path toward the next stage of human evolution. In the 1970s she cofounded the Committee for the Future in Washington, D.C., which developed the New Worlds Educational and Training Center based on her work. She coproduced twenty-five synergistic convergence (SYNCON) conferences to bring together people from every field and function to seek common goals and match needs and resources in the light of the growing-edge potentials of humanity. Her books include *Conscious Evolution: Awakening the Power of Our Social Potential, Emergence: The Shift from Ego to Essence, The Evolutionary Journey: Your Guide to a Positive Future,* and *Revelation: A Message of Hope for the New Millennium.*

Swami Kriyananda is one of the foremost proponents of yogic teachings in the world today. In 1948, at the age of twenty-two, he became a disciple of the Indian yoga master Paramhansa Yogananda. He is one of a few remaining direct disciples of Yogananda active today. At Yogananda's request, Swami Kriyananda has devoted his life to lecturing and writing, helping others to experience the living presence of God within. He has taught on four continents in seven languages over the course of over sixty years. His teaching, audio and video recordings of his talks and music, and his many books, which have been translated into twenty-eight languages, have touched the lives of millions. A monastic almost all of his adult life, Swami Kriyananda is a swami of the Giri (Mountain) branch of the ancient Swami Order, as was his guru and his guru's guru, Swami Sri Yukteswar. He is the spiritual guide of Ananda Sangha Worldwide.

Ervin Laszlo, Ph.D., is founder and president of the Club of Budapest, chancellor of Giordano Bruno GlobalShift University, founder and director of the General Evolution Research Group, fellow of the World Academy of Arts and Sciences, member of the International Academy of Philosophy of Science, senator of the International Medici Academy, member of the Hungarian Academy of Sciences, founding father of WorldShift International, and editor of the international periodical *World Futures: The Journal of Global Education.* He is the author or coauthor of fifty-nine books, which have been translated into as many as twenty-three languages, and the editor of another thirty volumes, including a four-volume encyclopedia. Ervin Laszlo has a Ph.D. degree from the Sorbonne and is the recipient of four honorary Ph.D. degrees (from the United States, Canada, Finland, and Hungary). He received the peace prize of Japan, the Goi Peace Award, in Tokyo in 2002 and the International Mandir of Peace Prize in Assisi in 2005. He was nominated for the Nobel Peace Prize in 2004 and was renominated in 2005. He presently lives in a three-hundred-year-old converted farmhouse in Tuscany.

Alison Rose Levy is a much-published writer with more than twenty years of experience creating communications for major media, focusing on integrative health, lifestyle, yoga, psychology, and spiritual transformation. Levy has written several *New York Times* bestsellers, working with physicians and medical experts. She also served as senior health editor of *New Age Journal* and was executive producer for Trinity Church in New York City. Levy has also produced prime-time cultural and news specials for PBS and the Smithsonian Institution. A New York native, Levy also draws on her wealth of health knowledge in her practice as a lifestyle coach and facilitator using the family constellations method.

Bruce Lipton, Ph.D., is an internationally recognized leader in bridging science and spirit. A stem cell biologist, the bestselling author of

The Biology of Belief, and a recipient of the 2009 Goi Peace Award, he has been a guest speaker on hundreds of TV and radio shows as well as the keynote presenter for national and international conferences. He began his scientific career as a cell biologist. He received his Ph.D. degree from the University of Virginia, in Charlottesville, before joining the Department of Anatomy at the University of Wisconsin's School of Medicine in 1973. His novel scientific approach transformed his personal life as well. His deepened understanding of cell biology highlighted his understanding of the mechanisms by which the mind controls bodily functions and implied the existence of an immortal spirit. He applied this science to his personal biology and discovered that his physical well-being improved and that the quality and character of his daily life was greatly enhanced.

Joanna Macy, Ph.D., is the primary source and root teacher of the "work that reconnects." The theory and practice of this group work are described on her website and in her book *Coming Back to Life.* Macy is an eco-philosopher and a scholar of Buddhism, general systems theory, and deep ecology. A respected voice in the movements for peace, justice, and ecology, she interweaves her scholarship with four decades of activism. She has created a groundbreaking theoretical framework for personal and social change as well as a powerful workshop methodology for its application. She travels widely, giving lectures, workshops, and trainings in North and South America, Europe, Asia, and Australia. She lives in Berkeley, California, near her children and grandchildren.

James O'Dea is currently lead faculty for the Peace Ambassador Training at the Shift Network where he has helped train five hundred students from thirty countries. He is a member of the extended faculty of the Institute of Noetic Sciences and its immediate past president. He was executive director of the Seva Foundation, an international health and development organization and for ten years was the Washington office director of Amnesty International. He is also an advisory board member of the Peace Alliance. Author of numerous essays, his book *Cultivating Peace* is scheduled for release in May 2012. His earlier work *Creative Stress: A Path For Evolving Souls Living Through Personal and Planetary Upheaval* (2010) has been highly praised.

Rustum Roy (July 3, 1924–August 26, 2010) was a materials scientist who held visiting professorships in materials science at Arizona State University and in medicine at the University of Arizona as well as an emeritus position at Pennsylvania State University in three departments. Roy was also intensely involved in reforming religious institutions— locally, nationally, and worldwide. The direction was always toward greater inclusiveness. He helped start what is one of the oldest ecumenical house churches in the country and was for thirty years on the board of the pioneering national ecumenical retreat center, Kirkridge. Since giving the prestigious Hibbert Lectures in London, incorporating the insights of science and technology into the world's religions, he has become a spokesman for a "radical pluralist" integration among the world's religions and cultures.

Peter Russell is a British writer and teacher living in Sausalito, California. His previous books include *The Global Brain, Waking Up in Time,* and most recently, *From Science to God: The Mystery of Consciousness and the Meaning of Light.* His principal interest is the deeper spiritual significance of the times we are passing through, and as one of the more revolutionary futurists, Russell has been a keynote speaker at many international conferences—in Europe, Japan, and the United States. Russell is a fellow of the Institute of Noetic Sciences, the World Business Academy, and the Findhorn Foundation and an honorary member of the Club of Budapest.

Masami Saionji is a descendant of the Royal Rykyu Family of Okinawa. Saionji has dedicated her life to the attainment and awakening of global consciousness for personal as well as planetary peace. She is regarded as a leader in the human potential movement and is highly respected as a spiritual teacher, both in Japan and throughout the world. She travels extensively on speaking tours and has led peace ceremonies on every continent and in major cities around the world. She has touched thousands of peoples' lives through her guidance and inspiration. Saionji also serves as chairperson of the Goi Peace Foundation and the Byakko Shinko Kai and is an honorary member of the Club of Budapest and the World Wisdom Council.

Marilyn Mandala Schlitz, Ph.D., is president and CEO of the Institute of Noetic Sciences, where she has worked for fifteen years. Her work focuses on psychophysiology, cross-cultural healing, and consciousness studies. She has given lectures, conducted workshops, and taught all around the country. She completed her training in psychology, behavioral and social sciences, and philosophy at Stanford University, University of Texas–San Antonio, and Wayne State University in Detroit. She received her Ph.D. degree in anthropology at the University of Texas–Austin. She has also authored and coauthored numerous books, such as *Living Deeply: The Art and Science of Transformation* and *Consciousness and Healing: Integral Approaches to Mind-Body Medicine.*

Sri Sri Ravi Shankar is a humanitarian leader, spiritual teacher, and ambassador of peace. His vision of a stress-free, violence-free society has united millions of people the world over through service projects and the courses of the Art of Living Foundation. Sri Sri has rekindled the traditions of yoga and meditation and offered them in a form that is relevant to the twenty-first century. Beyond reviving ancient wisdom, Sri Sri has created new techniques for personal and social transformation. His work has touched the lives of millions of people around the world, going beyond the barriers of race, nationality, and religion with the message of a "one-world family"; that inner and outer peace are possible; and that a stress-free, violence-free society can be created through service and the reawakening of human values.

Rabbi Awraham Soetendorp is an award-winning human rights advocate, lecturer, writer, environmental activist, and champion of a civil society worldwide who is active in a wide variety of progressive, humanitarian, and interfaith organizations and initiatives. Born in 1943 in Amsterdam, the Netherlands, Rabbi Soetendorp was saved by a righteous couple and survived as a "hidden child." He went on to receive his ordination from Leo Baeck College of London in 1967 and was instrumental in the reestablishment of Jewish communities in the Netherlands. He is the rabbi emeritus of Congregation Beth Jehuda in the Hague and former president of the European region of the World Union for Progressive Judaism. Rabbi Soetendorp is a founding member of the Islam and the West dialogue group, formerly C100, of the World Economic Forum. Rabbi Soetendorp and his wife, Sira, who is a child survivor and social worker, are blessed with two daughters and six grandchildren.

Shinichi Takemura is a media producer known for his numerous cutting-edge, information technology–driven social activities, along with propounding his incisive views as an anthropologist. Currently, he's a professor at Kyoto University of Art and Design, teaching anthropology, international relations, information society theory, and other subjects. Professor Takemura is engaged in the development of social information platforms, or what he calls "socialware," with the Earth Literacy Program, a nonprofit organization that he runs as a base for his activities. Professor Takemura is currently involved in the implementation of the "Global Corridor," which provides a channel for children in nations facing the informational divide, such as Afghanistan, Sri Lanka, Bangladesh, and Cambodia, and which aims to open up a path for such children to participate in the global society.

Hiroshi Tasaka is a Japanese poet, scientist, and distinguished economist. He teaches at Tama University in Tokyo. Since 2000 he has worked as an outside director and advisor for various firms in industries such as information, logistics, finance, education, and the environment. In 2001, he established his personal website called Wind from the Future, from which he sends out weekly e-mail messages, Message from the Wind, and airs the Internet radio program called *Conversation with the Wind,* to thirty thousand members. He has authored more than forty books on business strategies, the Internet revolution, and models of social change, and he is the founder of SophiaBank, a network of think tanks dedicated to fostering social entrepreneurs. He also serves as the president of the Club of Budapest, Japan.

Index

BOOKS OF RELATED INTEREST

Science and the Akashic Field
An Integral Theory of Everything
by Ervin Laszlo

The Akashic Experience
Science and the Cosmic Memory Field
by Ervin Laszlo

New Consciousness for a New World
How to Thrive in Transitional Times and Participate in the Coming
Spiritual Renaissance
by Kingsley L. Dennis

The Struggle for Your Mind
Conscious Evolution and the Battle to Control How We Think
by Kingsley L. Dennis

Morphic Resonance
The Nature of Formative Causation
by Rupert Sheldrake

The Biology of Transcendence
A Blueprint of the Human Spirit
by Joseph Chilton Pearce

The Basic Code of the Universe
The Science of the Invisible in Physics, Medicine, and Spirituality
by Massimo Citro, M.D.

New World Mindfulness
From the Founding Fathers, Emerson,
and Thoreau to Your Personal Practice
by Donald McCown and Marc S. Micozzi, M.D., Ph.D.

INNER TRADITIONS • BEAR & COMPANY
P.O. Box 388
Rochester, VT 05767
1-800-246-8648
www.InnerTraditions.com

Or contact your local bookseller